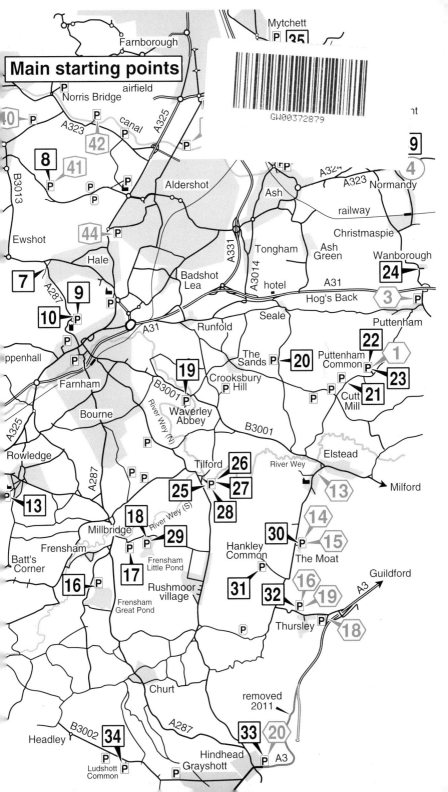

1 **Odiham and Roke Farm**

About 7 km/4¼ miles over rolling farm land. The extension of 1½ km/1 mile via the Basingstoke Canal and the short cut of 2¼ km/1½ miles can be used together. OS maps 1:25000 144 Basingstoke, 1:50000 186 Aldershot.

Start in Odiham. Park in London Road near High Street, SU 743 511. The extension passes Odiham Wharf car park, SU 747 517, Broad Oak car park, SU 753 520, and a large layby on the A287, SU 756 511.

Linking walks

3☆ 4✿ ㊷✪ ☒34☒ ✶ ☒35☒ ❀

The George ☎ 01256 702081
The Waterwitch ☎ 01256 702778
The Bell ☎ 01256 702282

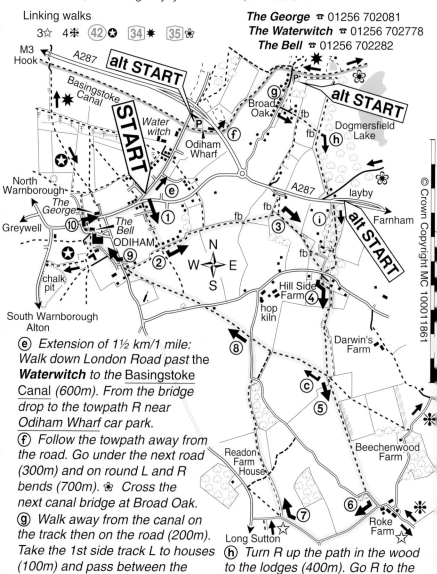

© Crown Copyright MC 100011861

ⓔ *Extension of 1½ km/1 mile: Walk down London Road past the* **Waterwitch** *to the* Basingstoke Canal *(600m). From the bridge drop to the towpath R near* Odiham Wharf *car park.*

ⓕ *Follow the towpath away from the road. Go under the next road (300m) and on round L and R bends (700m).* ❀ *Cross the next canal bridge at Broad Oak.*

ⓖ *Walk away from the canal on the track then on the road (200m). Take the 1st side track L to houses (100m) and pass between the gardens to the field (30m). Cross it slightly R into the wood (200m).*

ⓗ *Turn R up the path in the wood to the lodges (400m). Go R to the road (100m) and back L along the L verge to the layby (100m).*

2

(i) *Cross to Lotham's drive and take the path diverging L of it into the trees. When boggy go along the drive and take the winding path opposite the first house until the paths meet (outside a field corner) (300m). Continue on the main path bending R to the road (200m).* ➤(4)

(1) At the bottom of Odiham High Street, opposite the end of London Road, take the path between the houses up to the fields (300m).

(2) Turn L along the edge. Pass a side path L in the 2nd field, and keep on to the stream (600m). Cross the footbridge to the L field. Continue in the same direction, diverging from the R edge (170m).

(3) In the next field go L briefly (40m). Cross the ditch and hedge then turn R along the edge to the corner of the field (250m). In the next field follow the hedge R to the footbridge R (100m). Cross to the next field and aim diagonally L. Join the road via the drive (100m).

(4) Cross into the drive of Hillside Cottage and enter the field R. Look for the houses L and cross the little fields to the top (R) corner of the garden (120m). Turn R along the hedge (100m). Cross the hedge R but stay beside it. When it bends L, the right-of-way is ahead about 50m R of the hedge but the path is usually beside the hedge. Make for the protruding hedge corner where four paths meet (400m). ✳

(c) *Short cut of 2½ km/1½ miles: From the corner turn back R on the RoW down the field. Aim for the spiked tower (Odiham Church), on the next ridge, to a gateway, across the next field (600m) and over the road.* ➤(8)

(5) Cross the hedge at the corner. Go up beside it briefly and straight over to the next protruding hedge corner (150m) then on beside the L fence over the top. When the fence bends L (300m) go straight over the field to the gateway (400m) and along the road L to the bend at Roke Farm (100m). ☆

(6) Turn R on the concrete farm track. Keep on round the curve past the junction (400m) down to the L bend (300m).

(7) Turn R into the field. Don't follow the diagonal right of way down the field but go along the hedge (250m). Cross a track and go on at the R edge of the next field then up beside the wood to the road (700m). Walk on down the road. Watch out for a cross path halfway down (300m). Turn into the L field.

(8) Go down the field to meet the road 50m L of the house at the bottom (400m). Cross the road and go on up the next field on the same line and along the hedge of the sports field to the top L corner near the houses then out to the road (600m).

(9) A few paces up the road take the side road L & R to the church-yard (200m). ✪ The pest house is at the L corner. Cross past the tower of Odiham Church to the church square, The Borough. See the stocks R. Walk along the drive L of the **Bell** and on through the passageway to High Street (100m).

(10) Walk down the High Street R past the **George** (100m) ✿ and on to London Road (250m). Visualize how wide High Street would be without the parked cars.

2 Well to Long Sutton

About 7½ km/4¾ miles with an extension of 800 km/½ mile and a short cut of 800m/½ mile; mainly arable farmland, undulating; best when the crops are tall; muddy in winter. OS maps 1:25000 144 Basingstoke, 1:50000 186 Aldershot.

Start from Well, SU 760 466, or Long Sutton, SU 738 473. There is no large public parking place near the route. At Well park in the layby opposite *The Chequers*. At Long Sutton the village hall opposite the church has a car park.

Linking walks 3★ [30] ✦

The Chequers ☎ 01256 862605
The Four Horseshoes ☎ 01256 862488

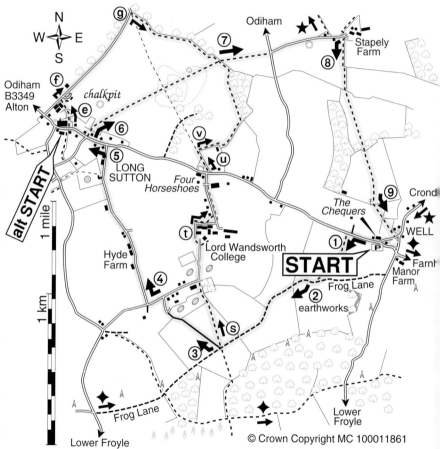

© Crown Copyright MC 100011861

① From the ***Chequers*** walk away from Well on the road towards Long Sutton (250m). Soon after the track between fields R watch out for a footpath L (30m) and cross the field slightly R down to the bottom edge, 150m from the R corner (400m).

② Join the track (Frog Lane) and follow it R. Watch out for a junction with a track R and paths (800m). ✦ The routes now follow rights-of-way through Lord Wandsworth College. RAF Odiham Airfield is visible northwards from the hilltop.

4

(S) *Short cut: Enter the field R and ascend diagonally to the top R corner, near the clump of trees. Cross the end of the sports field (350m). Go out to the tarmac drive (150m) and follow the drive ahead down to the buildings (300m).*

(t) *Just before the buildings cross L to the parallel drive skirting the buildings. Continue to a T-junction (100m). Follow the drive R (100m), take the footpath cutting the corner and walk down the main drive L and out at the main gate (300m). The* **Four Horseshoes** *is L 50m.*

(u) *Slightly R (30m) take the path on the other side, along the hedge to a re-entrant corner (150m).*

(v) *Turn R. Keep to the edge of the field past the wood (850m). After the wood (100m) turn R.* →(7)

(3) Turn R up the track between fields. On top continue on the drive to the T-junction (600m).

(4) Turn L (120m) then R and carry on all the way down to the gate in Long Sutton (1100m).

(5) Walk through the village L to see the church and pond (350m).

(e) *Extension of ½ mile: Take the path across the churchyard and the small fields to the next lane (200m).*

(f) *Follow the lane R (700m).*

(g) *Just before the L bend turn into the field R and follow the winding L edge almost to the wood (700m). Turn L.* →(7)

(6) Return along the road (250m). Opposite Wingate Lane, take the track between gardens (50m). Go on at the L edge of the field (50m) then bear R up over the middle. If the path is unclear, aim over the high point, and 100m L of the wood beyond it, to the edge (900m).

(7) In the next field bear R aiming for the distant hilltop (Horsedown Common) until you see the exit to the road junction (450m). Cross the road and continue on the lane ahead past the cottage L ★ to the end at Stapely Farm (500m).

(8) When the lane splits, turn R up into the field and follow the L edge down to the bottom (400m). Cross the next field ahead up the middle of the slight valley parallel with the edge of the wood and into a bend in the hedge (400m). In the third field make for the stile at the middle of the top edge (400m).

(9) In the next field cross the L corner to the hedge-end (100m). Go up past the hedge corner and ahead to the road (200m. Turn R for the *Chequers* (100m).

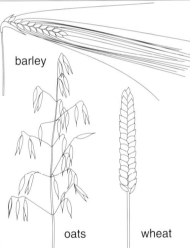

barley

oats   wheat

The chief cereals grown in the south of England are wheat, barley and oats. Some varieties of wheat have awns (bristles) but the heads do not "nod" like barley and the awns are not as long. Cereals are grasses cultivated for their seeds. These are products of about eight millennia of cultivation but not closely related.

3 Well, Roke Farm and Horsedown Common

About 7 km/4½ miles with extensions of 3 km/1¾ miles and 1 km/¾ mile; undulating farm country. The lanes are good for varying the route. OS maps 1:25000 144 Basingstoke, 1:50000 186 Aldershot.

Start at Well. Park in the layby opposite the pub, SU 760 466.

Linking walks
1☆ 2★ 4✿ ⟨30⟩ ✿

The Chequers
☎ 01256 862605

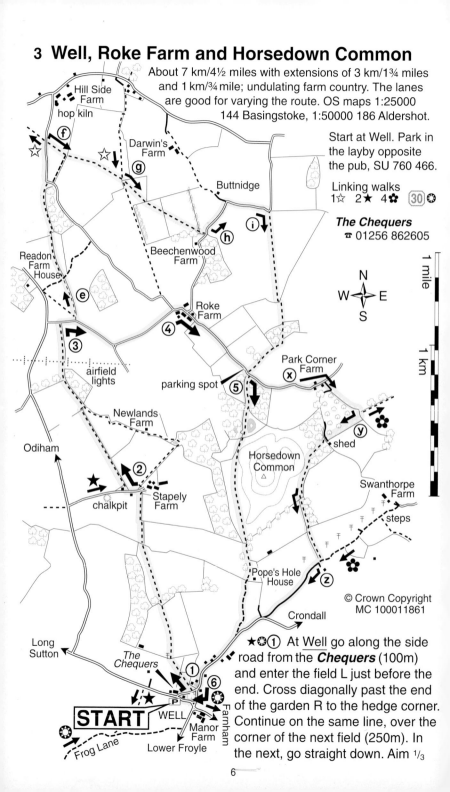

© Crown Copyright
MC 100011861

★✿① At Well go along the side road from the **Chequers** (100m) and enter the field L just before the end. Cross diagonally past the end of the garden R to the hedge corner. Continue on the same line, over the corner of the next field (250m). In the next, go straight down. Aim ⅓ of the way across the bottom edge from the wood to cross the stile on the protruding corner (400m). Keep on parallel with the edge of the wood (400m), up the R edge of the next field to the top (400m) and out R to Stapely Farm.

② Go L along the lane away from the farm (100m). Turn off at the 1st garden R and carry on along the R edge of the fields then beside the wood and down under the flight path of Odiham Airfield (1000m) to the concrete farm drive (300m).

ⓔ *Extension of 3 km/1¾ miles: Turn R up to the bend (100m) then L. Don't follow the right of way diagonally down the field but walk beside the hedge (250m). Cross a track and go on at the R edge of the fields then up beside the wood to the road (700m). Walk on down the road watching out for a path crossing halfway down (300m).*

ⓕ *Climb the R bank and go over the field to the gap in the hedge (150m). Look ahead. The next hedge crosses round the top of the hill. Aim for the L end where it meets the uphill hedge (450m).*

ⓖ *Just before the corner cross the top hedge at the projecting bend. Don't follow the right-of-way up beside it but the diverging one to the furthest corner (200m). Keep on in the same line over the fields to the top corner between trees (500m). Exit across the narrow end of the next field (30m).*

ⓗ *Follow the road down L (300m), round the R bend and on as far as the next (L) bend (300m).*

ⓘ *Turn R up the field. Aim for the top point in the wood above it. At the top of the converging L edge*

(600m) *take the path between the fields, through the wood, round a R bend (300m) and up to the road (350m).* ♦⑤ *across or* ♦ⓧ *L*

③ Go up the drive. Avoid a branch R and keep on to the farm (700m).

④ Follow the road round through Roke Farm and carry on between fields to the wood R (700m).

ⓧ *Extension of 1 km/¾ mile: Stay on the road to Park Corner Farm (600m). Turn R up the track after the last house (80m). When it bends R go straight on through the field next to the R fence (200m).* ♣

ⓨ *Go on into the next field (40m) then cross the ditch R into the plantation and follow the L edge (300m). Cross the track into the wood and bear slightly L on the path through the wood to the foot of the hill at Horsedown Common (150m). Bear L around the foot (200m). Just over the footbridge exit L along the edge of the wood and carry on down the R edge of the next field to the track (400m).*

ⓩ *Follow the track R to the end (500m) and go on along the road to Well (650m).* ♦⑥

⑤ Take the path along the edge of the wood and into the corner of the field of Horsedown Common (hill) (200m). Keep straight on, skirting round the lower slopes over several fences aiming for the far R corner with the hedge (900m). Exit 30m L of the corner along the path in the belt of trees to Pope's Hole House (250m). Go on along the track to the road (400m) then along the road to Well (400m).

⑥ Just after the pond R don't fork R but go on to the well (100m) then R to the *Chequers* (100m).

4 Crondall to Horsedown Common

About 8 km/5 miles with an extension of 1½ km/1 mile; undulating farmland; long views; nice in winter but boggy in wet years; sporadic shade in summer. OS maps 1:25000 144 Basingstoke, 1:50000 186 Aldershot.

Start at Crondall, SU 794 485; park beside the churchyard wall.

Linking walks 1✳ 3✿ 5✳ 6✦ 38✿

The Plume of Feathers 01252 850245
The Hampshire Arms 01252 850418

Roke Farm

Park Corner Farm

1 km   1 mile

N
W E
S

(g) (h)

(10)

shed

Horsedown Common
△

Swanthorpe Farm

fb (9)

steps

(7)

(8)

Pope's Hole House

(e)

(6)

Traver's Farm

(f)

Well

✦① From Crondall Church follow Croft Lane out of the village to the R bend (400m).
② Don't go round the bend but take the track ahead (40m) and turn L below the barn. Carry on up the field round R & L bends (400m) and on (250m).
③ Turn R on the track over the field to the wood (450m) and stay on the track up through the trees (200m). ✳
④ When it curves slightly R to the corner of the field, take the side path R inside the edge of the wood (200m). Emerging at the corner of the wood carry on ahead beside the L hedge all the way to the road (400m).
⑤ Go L either on the road or on the path beside it, which rejoins the lane at the end of the wood and restarts in the next field. At the side road (350m) carry on ahead to the first house R (200m).
⑥ Next to the drive follow the path around the curving edge of the field (600m). At the bottom of the slope, where the hedge bends L, cut straight over the field to the dip in the far edge and drop down steps to the sunken track (150m).
⑦ Go L up the sunken track until it is level with the fields below the hill, Horsedown Common (550m).

(e) Extension of 1½ km/1 mile: Go on to the end of the track (500m) and ahead on the road (200m). ✿
(f) Turn back R on the next track (350m). After the house continue on the footpath through the trees (200m) and ahead in the field with the hill. Diverge very slightly from the L edge skirting round the lower slopes and crossing several fences. Eventually join the wooded edge of the field into the L corner (700m) and carry on out along the path through the trees to the road (350m). ✳

(g) *Follow the road R and down past Park Corner Farm (600m).*

(h) *Turn R into the field after the last house. Don't follow the track bend R but stay ahead through the field at the R edge (350m). Pass into the next field then turn L.* →(10)

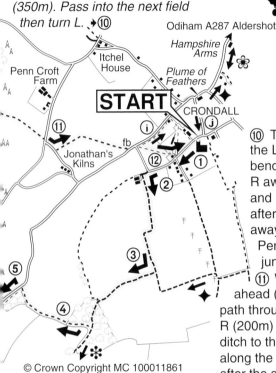

Odiham A287 Aldershot

Hampshire Arms

Plume of Feathers

Itchel House

Penn Croft Farm

START

CRONDALL

(i)

(j)

(11)

fb

Jonathan's Kilns

(12)

(1)

(2)

(3)

(5)

(4)

© Crown Copyright MC 100011861

Chinook

(10) The right of way is beside the L edge until the hedge bends L (300m). Then it turns R away from the hedge (40m) and L, parallel with the hedge after which it gradually curves away R. Follow it down below Penn Croft Farm to the road junction (850m).

(11) Walk down the road ahead (100m) then turn L on the path through the field which bends R (200m) and eventually crosses a ditch to the next road (300m). Walk along the road L and into the field R after the side road R (50m).

(i) *If going to the **Feathers** carry straight on along the edge of the field next to the road (300m) then on the road itself (200m).* ❀

(j) *Return to Croft Lane via Church Street (300m).*

(8) Just before a side track L, enter the field R and go up the R side of the hedge (250m). At the top carry on through the edge of the wood, out to the foot of the hill (200m).

(9) Go R, over the footbridge and follow the fence. When it bends R (100m) carry on briefly outside the trees then bear R down through the trees to the fence (200m). The stile is 50m beyond a shed in the adjacent field. Exit from the wood and go straight on near the R edge of the plantation (300m) and ahead in the next field.

(12) Go up the diagonal path from the corner to the top edge near a garden hedge (200m). Pass into the next field and go over the grass to the far R corner of the cricket pitch (200m) and out to Croft Lane near the churchyard.

5 Crondall to Montgomery's Farm

About 8 km/5 miles with a short cut of 1 km/¾ mile; undulating farmland; long views; a good winter walk with traffic-free lanes. OS maps 1:25000 144 Basingstoke, 1:50000 186 Aldershot.

Start at Crondall Church, SU 794 485; park beside the churchyard wall.

Linking walks   4❖   6✳   ③①✳   ③⑧✧

Plume of Feathers 01252 850245
Hampshire Arms 01252 850418

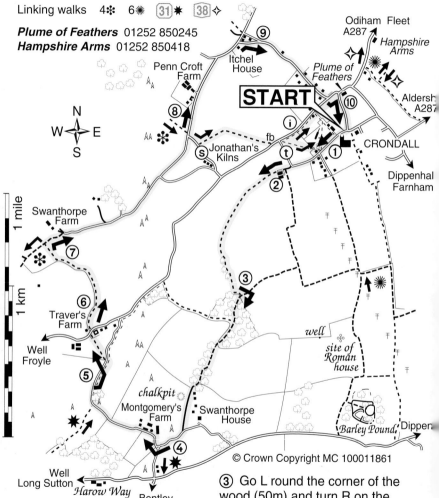

© Crown Copyright MC 100011861

✳① From Crondall Church walk along the L edge of the cricket field beside Croft Lane (150m) then on the lane until it bends R (250m).

② Go up the track ahead (50m). Don't turn L just before the barns but go past them and up the curving path to the wood (1050m).

③ Go L round the corner of the wood (50m) and turn R on the track. Keep on up through the wood (300m) then up the R edge of the field and through the trees between fields (400m). Emerging at houses, carry on up the drive beside the field to the road (250m).

④ Go R to the end of the road ✳ (250m) then R again down past

Montgomery's Farm (200m) and past a path from L near the pylon R (350m). Stay on the road until past the trees (chalkpit) R (150m) then enter the field R. Carry on beside the road watching for a gap in the hedge at a footpath over the road (200m). (If you miss this path go down the edge to the bottom (300m) then along the road L to the 1st house R (300m).)

⑤ Go down the footpath L to the road (200m) then R to the house drive on the opposite side (40m).

⑥ Next to the drive follow the path around the curving edge of the field (600m). At the bottom of the slope, where the hedge bends L, cut straight over the field to the dip in the far edge and drop down the steps to the track (150m). ❋

⑦ Walk down the sunken track R (100m) and along the narrow road between fields, past the first side road R and on to the 2nd (1150m).

Ⓢ *Short cut of 1 km/¾ mile: Start down the side road R (100m) then turn off L through the field on the path which bends R (200m) and eventually crosses a ditch to the next road (300m). Turn L along the road to the side road R (50m).*

ⓘ *If going to the **Feathers** carry on along the field above the road (300m) then on the road (200m).*

ⓣ *After the side road go up the diagonal path from the corner to the top edge near a garden hedge (200m). Cross into the next field and go straight on over the grass to the far R corner of the cricket field (200m) and out to Croft Lane near the churchyard.*

⑧ Stay on the road up round the side of the valley past the farm (300m) and a side road L (300m) to Itched House R (200m).

⑨ Turn R down the side lane to Crondall (750m).

⑩ At the bottom turn L to the **Feathers** (100m) ✧ then R up Church Street (300m).

Rape provides farmers with a crop break, fields with colour and walkers with horror stories of blocked paths. After flowering it is recognized by its height, 1½m, and numerous pods. The seedlings look like cabbages as might be expected for rape is another Brassica (*B. napus*). A good crop is 3½ tons of seed per acre/8 tonnes per hectare. Oil yield is almost 50%.

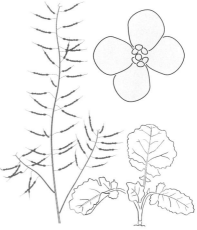

In Britain, farmers have a choice of about 60 varieties. Winter rape (sown August, cut July) and Spring rape (sown April /May, cut September) can be harvested by combine before and after the cereals. The oil of high erucic acid (C22:1) varieties finds industrial use as a slip agent for polythene and a 2-stroke lubricant and is converted in burgeoning quantities into a diesel substitute. The 00 varieties are used by food manufacturers for margarine, cooking oil and animal meal. New varieties are being developed, rich in fatty acids for specific uses.

6 Crondall, Dora's Green and Wimble Hill

About 8 km/5 miles; over undulating fields with fine views; good in winter but sticky mud in wet years. OS maps 1:25000 144+145, 1:50000 186 Aldershot.

Start at Crondall Church, SU 794 485; park beside the churchyard wall.

Linking walks   4✦   5✳   7❀   9★   11✿   38 ❀

The Plume of Feathers 01252 850245   ***The Hampshire Arms*** 01252 850418

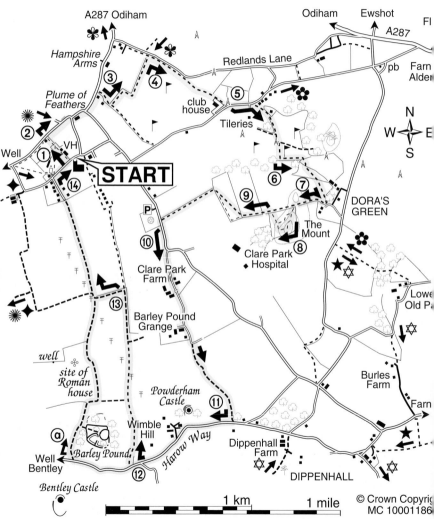

© Crown Copyright
MC 10001186

① From Crondall Church enter the cricket field and walk down the R edge to the next road (200m).

② On the road go R (the pond L is the start of the River Hart) to the

Plume of Feathers (200m) and ahead along The Borough and Pankridge Street (250m).

③ At the first field R, walk up the the R edge (100m) into the golf course then L at the edge, with R & L turns, to the next road (550m). ❧

④ Follow the path R above the road (400m). When the road bends away L, bear R along the edge of the golf course into the corner of the car park. Join the road (300m).

⑤ Walk up the road L (200m). ❀ At Tileries turn off R between the gardens. Continue along the R edge then straight over the golf course past the pylon (450m).

⑥ At the far edge, turn L (100m) and enter the small field R. Cross the corner (50m) then aim diagonally L up the next field over the brow into the top field (100m).

⑦ Cross the L corner of the field towards the houses of Dora's Green (150m).★✿ Don't go out to the drive but turn back R with the hedge up the slope (200m).

⑧ Just after the field entrance L on the crest, go L up through the plantation to the top of the Mount (200m) then R back down to the hedge and out (200m). Clare Park Hospital is visible below L.

⑨ Continue down beside the hedge (200m). At the flat field, make for the diagonally opposite corner. The right of way is diagonal but when muddy there is usually a path round the L edge (300m). Before the end exit L along the footpath to the road (400m).

⑩ Walk along the road L (200m). When it bends L continue ahead up the drive past Clare Park Farm. When the drive bends L (600m) go straight on up the track over the ridge to the road (600m).

⑪ Turn R and follow the road up (on the line of the Harow Way with Powderham Castle visible in winter as a mound in the trees above R) past Wimble Hill hamlet R and side road L (600m) and on.

ⓐ *Slightly longer alternative: Stay on the lane (400m) then take the track R. A side track into the wood R leads to* Barley Pound. ↳⑭

⑫ After the side road L (100m), climb the R bank to follow the footpath up the edge of the field over Wimble Hill. Stay ahead on the track from the farm R (1100m).

⑬ At the bottom corner disregard the path ahead. Go round the L bend along the hedge (200m) ✦❋ then turn R to Crondall (700m).

⑭ At the lane stay ahead (200m). Go R on Croft Lane or along the cricket field to the church (200m).

Barley Pound is a group of earth fortifications, deriving its name from the Domesday Book manor of BEDDELEIE, later called Badley then Clare Park. It is a Norman castle and the only one in Hampshire that cannot be related to historical events. Obligingly, there is a documented castle which has not been located. *Gesta Stephani* (The Deeds of Stephen) records that in 1147, during the war of succession between Stephen and Mathilda, a castle called *Lidelea* was captured from the Bishop of Winchester (Stephen's brother) and that he set up two siege castles in order to recover it. **Powderham Castle**, a motte (earth fort with central mound) and another now almost ploughed away, in the fields down towards Bentley, accord with this scenario. Did a catarrhal monk cause *Beddeleië* to mutate to *Lidelea* when dictating for copyists or did bad writing convert a Normanised *Bidelea* in an age of unfixed spelling?

Lidelea Castle - a suggested identification King & Renn Antiquaries Journal Vol 51 1971
Background to the three castles Bill Andrews *Crondall Society News* Spring 1997

7 Ewshot, Beacon Hill and Dora's Green.

About 10½ km/6½ miles; heath and farmland; an intricate route; avoidable boggy bits in winter; splendid views. OS maps 1:25000 145 Guildford, 1:50000 186 Aldershot.

Start at Ewshot village hall, SU 816 502, or from the roadside in Heathyfields Road, Upper Hale, SU 830 490.

Linking walks
6❀ 8❋ 9❋
39❖ 41❋ 44❋

START
EWSHOT

The Windmill
☎ 01252 850439

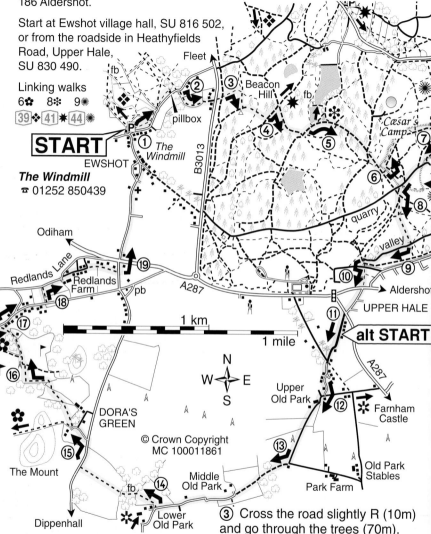

© Crown Copyright
MC 100011861

❖① From Ewshot walk along Tadpole Lane, or the fields L of it, to the pillbox on the L bank (500m).
② Just round the bend in the lane after the pillbox take the path R up the edge of the fields round to the house (250m). Exit past the garden to the road (fast traffic) (100m).

③ Cross the road slightly R (10m) and go through the trees (70m). Cross the track and follow the duct of the Army waterworks (150m). After the R curve cross the culvert and climb the steep path to the flat top of Beacon Hill (100m).
④ A vehicle track comes past the trig point to end on the corner of the plateau. Drop off this corner on the

14

steep stony path, down over the water duct to the hard track (150m). Turn L down to the cross track (100m). ✳ Take the track back R over a rise and down to the next track junction on a bend (300m).

⑤ Turn L down the track past the end of the reservoirs L (150m). ❖ Keep on round the R curve and up to a major track descending L (450m). Just after it (20m) turn L up the side track (200m).

⑥ On the brow of the hill turn L through the Iron Age ramparts of Cæsar's Camp. Walk all the way round the scarp edge (650m). ✳

⑦ Don't descend the last steep stony path but go R on the level track until it joins the major vehicle track (200m) then R (250m).

⑧ At the next cross track turn L. Very soon (50m) fork R then L to the edge of the hill (130m). Go on down into the valley (400m).

⑨ Either follow the valley track up R or climb the valley side to the next ridge track (150m) and go R to where these tracks almost meet at their ends (350m).

⑩ Pass through the gate L at the notch in the boundary mound. Cross the track on the other side and, slightly L, follow the small path ahead past the playing field to the main road (150m). Go down Lawday Link (200m) to Heathyfields Road.

⑪ From the top of Heathyfields Road walk down to the cluster of houses at the end (500m). ✳

⑫ Just before the end fork R to the next group of houses (100m). Go R at the track, round the L bend at Upper Old Park Farm and down between the fields (500m).

⑬ At the L bend and house, go R down the side track into the valley (200m) and up to Middle Old Park (200m). Carry on along the tarmac past Keeper's Cottage to Lower Old Park Farm (600m).

⑭ When the road bends L enter the field R. Skirt round the corner of the garden and cut across the L corner of the field to the wood (150m). Go down into the wood, over the brook and up to the next field (100m). Walk straight ahead up the field to exit at the highest point (350m).

⑮ Walk down the road R (200m). Just round the bend turn L up the side lane (150m). ❖ Just before the houses L take the path R into the field (20m). Follow the R edge briefly and then cross the corner to the edge under the trees (150m). Descend the next small field aiming for the bottom L corner (100m). Cross the footbridge and the next little field to the golf course (50m).

⑯ Follow the hedge L (100m) then turn R across the golf course past the pylon to the hedge corner (200m). Stay ahead beside the hedge and out between gardens to the road at Tileries (250m).

⑰ Walk up the road R (350m).

⑱ After the last house R take the footpath L down into the fields and up to Redlands Lane (100m). Walk up the lane R (150m). On the bend diverge R on the track past the houses of Warren Corner and go on up the path to the road (350m).

⑲ Turn L to the main road and cross (100m). Go on along the lane past Ewshot Church (500m) and down to the **Windmill** (200m) and the village hall (200m).

8 Cæsar's Camp and the Wellington Statue

About 7 km/4½ miles with a steep extension of 1 km/¾ mile over Beacon Hill. Entirely on heath; splendid views; army training land but open to the public; good in winter. OS maps 1:25000 145 Guildford, 1:50000 186 Aldershot.

Start from Bourley Road car park, SU 831 510, in the dip near Bourley Lane. There are other parking areas to confuse with it.

Linking walks 7 ✽ 41 ☆ 44 ✦

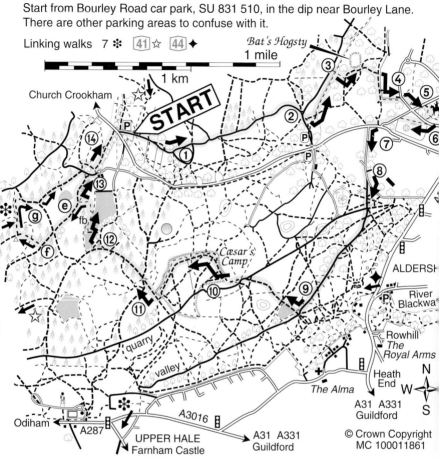

① From the top of the Bourley Road car park walk up the main track. After the bend near the top of the first rise (300m) don't fork R but stay on the main track, which undulates and winds past numerous cross tracks. Eventually descend in a broad R curve to a T-junction (1000m).

② Turn L, not on the hard track but the soft track beyond it (40m). Cross Claycart Stream (60m) and turn L along the little path beside it. Watch for a water chute L (250m).

③ Soon after the chute (70m) turn off R on the path up through the wood to the next track (100m) then L past the fence of Bat's Hogsty (100m). Keep on round the bend to the end (200m).

④ Follow the boundary track R to the corner of the fence (170m) and take the small path L beside the fence to the road (150m).

16

⑤ It is possible to cut the corner through the heath and trees but safer to go R to the crossroads (100m) and on (100m) watching out for a path L up the hillock L to the Wellington Statue. ✦
After a close-up view go back down towards the Garrison church.
⑥ Walk away from the church around the end of the hillock (100m) then cross the road L and cut through the football field (200m). Rejoin the road and go L to the T-junction (150m).
⑦ Go R along the verge (100m) then cross to the concrete army track. Follow it up (350m).
⑧ When the concrete starts to curve L, fork R on the hard track which soon passes between hillocks and down into a dip. Stay on this undulating track until level with the pond R (1000m).
⑨ Turn R across the end of the pond and the dam. Disregard side paths and continue up the hillside to the next hard track (400m).
⑩ Start up the track L but almost immediately (30m) branch off up the steep pebbly path to Cæsar's Camp (100m). Follow the edge of the scarp all the way round until it fades into the hill (700m). ❇
⑪ Just round a L bend in the path turn R through the ramparts (40m). then R over the brow of the hill. Drop steeply to the track junction (200m). Turn down (30m) and fork L to the Army waterworks reservoir ponds (450m). ☆
⑫ Leave the track and walk R of the water (100m), L over the dam (100m) and on beside the second reservoir to the side path up L half-way along (150m). Go up over the little hill, round L and down to the track (150m).
ⓔ *Extension via* Beacon Hill*: Go L to the track junction (250m) and ahead up the major track (100m).*
ⓕ *Turn R up the steep path to the brow of Beacon Hill (150m). Start towards the trig point (20m) then find the small path back R dropping off the hill steeply. Follow it down. Eventually it curls R to join a track (250m).*
ⓖ *Carry on down to the junction (50m) then L down on the hard track (350m). At the bottom cross into the field (50m).* ➔⑭
⑬ Follow the track down R to the bottom (200m). Turn R on the bottom track but watch out for a footbridge L (70m) and cross it.
⑭ Follow the track round the R edge of the field to the road (300m) and cross to the car park.

The **Wellington Statue** arrived in this position in 1885. The bronze is from guns captured at Waterloo - about 40 tons. The statue has always been controversial. There were objections to commemorating Wellington when it was erected in 1846. There were objections when it was removed from Hyde Park corner for road widening in 1882. Currently objectors believe such a splendid statue should stand in a more public place.

The Wellington Military Memorial 1885-1985
Tim Childerhouse Southern Books 1985

The Duke of Wellington, 1769-1852, was born Arthur Wellesley, 3rd son of Garett, 1st Earl of Mornington. He joined the army in 1787 and reached the pinnacle of fame by his defeat of Napoleon at Waterloo. As a young man he had been an MP in the Irish Parliament. As an old man he was PM in the British Parliament and ultimately loathed.

9 Farnham Old Park

About 6½ km/4 miles with a short cut of 1½ km/1 mile; over undulating farmland and past Farnham Castle; good in winter though muddy in places.
OS maps 1:25000 145 Guildford, 1:50000 186 Aldershot.

Start from Farnham Park car park, SU 837 475.

Linking walks   6★   7✳   10✪   11◇

Golf Course Café ☎ 01252 715216
The Nelson Arms ☎ 01252 716078
Farnham Castle ☎ 01252 721194
The Keep (EH) ☎ 01252 713393

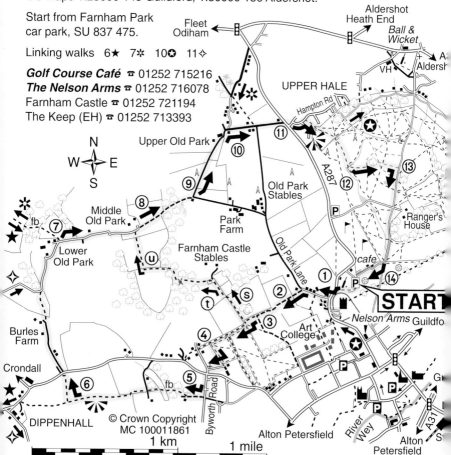

① From Farnham Park car park follow the edge of the cricket field round clockwise to the road (moat and curtain wall behind the trees) (200m). Go down the hill L (100m). On the bend notice Old Park Lane R but carry on (80m) and L into Farnham Castle. Cross the yard to the keep & inner court yard (100m). Return to Old Park Lane (over the road a path cuts the corner)(150m) and follow it to the R bend (200m).

② Turn L, between gardens, into the field and follow the track at the R edge to the L bend (450m).
⑤ *Short cut of 1½ km/1 mile: Turn R up the footpath beside the hedge (350m).*
① *At the top don't go on along the track ahead but turn L to the trees (50m). The path drops to a brook (150m) then winds R, L up to a field (150m). Walk up the R edge, halfway to the end (150m).*

18

ⓤ *Turn into the field R and go straight over towards the house (250m). On the lane turn R.* ➔⑧

③ Zigzag L,R round the protruding corner of the field (20m) and carry on. The main path is between hedges but enter the field L and walk along the hedge, and likewise in the next field (250m).

④ Turn L down beside the end hedge to the next corner and exit R to the lane (150m). Go R to the end (100m), over the main road and along Byworth Road to the third side road L (200m).

⑤ Opposite Waynflete Lane turn R along the track (50m) and bear R on the path in the trees (100m). Drop down to the narrow field and rise on the other side to the farm track (200m). Enter the field ahead and follow the top edge (100m). Climb the lynchet into the field L above but keep on in the same direction (hedge R) then along the middle of the ridge (400m). ★✧

⑥ Opposite the wooded side valley R take the side path R down off the ridge to the road (200m). Slightly L (10m) go up the R track opposite past houses (400m). When the track bends L up to the last house, keep on along the footpath ahead between the fields (200m). On the lane cross the bridge and climb out of the valley, skirting Lower Old Park (350m). ✲

⑦ On top, follow the R bend and go past Keeper's Cottage down to Middle Old Park (600m).

⑧ When the tarmac ends, stay ahead down the track into the valley and up to a house (400m).

⑨ Go L up the vehicle track from the bend (500m).

⑩ Just after the next house, at Upper Old Park, go round the R bend and on along the unmade road to the main road (400m).

⑪ Cross into Drovers Way (100m) and turn down Hampton Road (100m). Just after Blenheim Crescent, take the path R between the gardens (100m). ✪ 〽️

> **View** from the top of Farnham Park: On the line between the two nearest pylons, Crooksbury Hill and the nearby telecommunications tower should be visible. Behind the R pylon the knobbly hump is Gibbet Hill on the Greensand promontory stretching S to Blackdown. Behind the L pylon the distant steep edge is the escarpment of Leith Hill. Closer, the Hog's Back chalk ridge rises L behind this pylon. On very clear days the grandstand at Epsom Racecourse is visible along the N Downs. Farnham Castle is on the same chalk ridge, separated from the Hog's Back by low ground which was the valley of the Blackwater River. The ends of the ridge are misaligned by a horizontal fault which may be why the Ice Age rivers breached the chalk barrier here. The valley visible over the town R contains the River Wey (N) from Alton, once a tributary of the Blackwater.

Go straight down into Farnham Park, 50m L of the nearest pylon (200m). Just after the ditch, fork L over the rise (150m)

⑫ After the next ditch, bear L up the side path over the top, R of the clump of trees, and down to the tarmac path (350m).

⑬ Turn R. Follow the tarmac path over the drive of Ranger's House (250m), down in the valley (200m) and up through a hedge (150m).

⑭ Turn R along the hedge, past the football pavilion & ***Golf Course Café*** to the car park (200m).

10 Farnham Park and town

About 6 km/4 miles with an extension of 1½ km/1 mile; over undulating parkland and through the old part of the town. At certain times the Castle and Keep can be visited. OS maps 1:25000 145 Guildford, 1:50000 186 Aldershot.

Start from Farnham Park car park, SU 837 475, or Oast House Lane at Hale, SU 846 485, or The Green at Upper Hale, SU 842 489.

Linking walks
9❂ 19☆

Golf Course Café ☎ 01252 715216
Shepherd & Flock ☎ 01252 716675
William Cobbett ☎ 01252 726281
Nelson Arms ☎ 01252 716078
Six Bells ☎ 01252 716697

© Crown Copyright
MC 100011861

ⓘ *If starting at Oast House Lane go straight out over Farnham Park, R of the power lines and down round the first pylon (200m).* ➔⑦

❂① From the car park take the tarmac path into <u>Farnham Park</u> beside the golf club hedge, past the *café* and football pavilion (200m).

② At the T-junction go L down the tarmac path into the dip and up past the swallow hole to the drive from Ranger's House (350m).

③ Turn L along the drive L almost to the pond (170m) then take the path R beside the little valley to the hedge corner (250m). Stay ahead R of the pylon, over the stream (200m) and straight up the slope to the garden fences (100m).

④ Turn round for the view then descend diagonally L towards the corner near the wood (100m). Halfway down bear L into the wood and cross the Nadder Stream (100m).

20

⑤ Don't join the tarmac path but turn R beside the stream out of the trees (70m) then L up the little side path. Stay near the wood over a little stream and the ridge with several cross paths, then drop to the next stream (400m). Cross and fork R over the tarmac path (50m).
⑥ Keep on in the same direction, across another stream (60m) and round towards the pylon (150m). *(For Oast House Lane, exit up L.)*
⑦ At the pylon drop to the bottom of the valley (60m). Over the brook turn L along the valley side (150m). At the uphill hedge stay ahead over the stream then beside the cattle fence bending L to a pond (300m) then R to the end (200m). Cross the field up to the avenue (100m).
ⓔ *Extension of 1½ km/1 mile: Turn L along the avenue to the tarmac path (100m), then R to the corner of the park (100m) and L to the **Six Bells** (200m).*
ⓕ *Cross the road and Roman Way into the tarmac drive. Keep on down to* Bourne Mill *(400m).*
ⓖ *Cross Guildford Road and go L through the underpass to the **Shepherd & Flock** (100m). Walk down the lane, under road and rail bridges (300m), and on (200m).* ☆
ⓗ *Turn R on the drive to* High Mill *(100m). Over the bridge stay on the level winding path around the Wey Valley (700m). After the railway follow the track L, past a river bend (400m) and a cross path (100m) to the petrol station gate (100m).*
ⓚ *Cut through the petrol station and cross the dual carriageway to the path just L of Hatch Mill (80m). Follow the path down over the river (50m) and turn L.* ➧⑩

⑧ Turn R along the avenue (100m) then L over the grass to the children's play area (150m). Walk down the adjacent street (St James Avenue) to the traffic lights (250m).
⑨ Cross both roads. Go L down Guildford Road (100m) and R on Kimber's Lane to the end (100m). Keep on ahead along the path to the River Wey then beside it. Disregard the first bridges L (300m).
⑩ Stay on the bank to the next footbridge (200m). Cross the river but continue beside it (250m), over South Street and through the park (200m). After the footbridge aim for the road bridge.
⑪ Go over the river (50m), round the bend at the ***William Cobbett*** and R on Red Lion Lane (120m).
⑫ Turn R between the Maltings and car park (100m). Cross the footbridge and turn L. Cross the next car park to the vehicle exit (150m). Walk L along the road and through the churchyard (200m). ✡
⑬ Go clockwise round the church and out via Church Passage to West Street (100m). Cross.
⑭ Go along the street R (100m) then L through the arch and up the Lion & Lamb Yard to the supermarket at the top (100m).
⑮ Turn R and go out along the lane to Castle Street (150m). Walk up L past the ***Nelson Arms***. On the R side, after the houses, ascend the steps beside the road (400m).
⑯ Climb towards the gatehouse of Farnham Castle then join the drive into the courtyard to see the keep. Leave by the other drive L (100m) and continue up the road to the cricket field R. Skirt round R of the pitch to the car park (300m).

11 Dippenhall and the River Wey

About 7½ km/4¾ miles; undulating; boggy in wet seasons; overgrown paths in summer, lots of stiles. OS maps 1:25000 145 + 144, 1:50000 186 Aldershot.

Park on the stretch of old road next to *The Bull*, SU **803 443**, at crossroads on the A31. The sports field car parks at Wrecclesham are near the route.

Linking walks 6✿ 9✧ 12☆ 13✳

The Bull
☎ 01420 22156
The Royal Oak
☎ 01252 728319

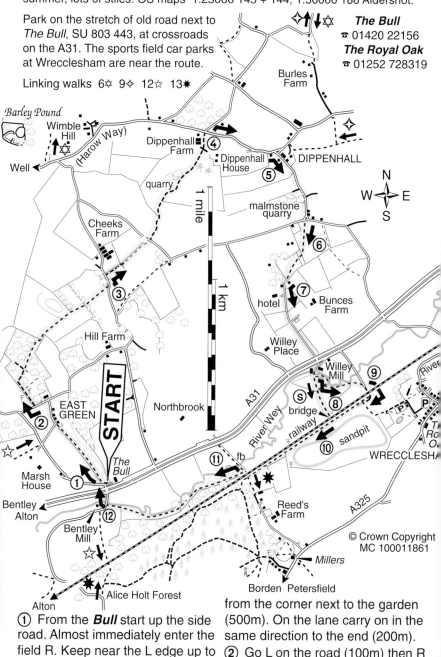

① From the *Bull* start up the side road. Almost immediately enter the field R. Keep near the L edge up to the houses at East Green and exit

from the corner next to the garden (500m). On the lane carry on in the same direction to the end (200m).
② Go L on the road (100m) then R along the track at the edge of the

wood (200m). Disregard all side tracks but when the track bends R follow it across the wood (350m). At the end take a few paces R to the corner (20m) and cross the ditch. Go on to the end of the hedge and straight up over the flank of the hill aiming for the R end of the trees on the flank. Keep on up to the road (500m). ✿

③ Start up the road L (70m) but turn off along the 1st cart track R. When it enters the field (150m) keep on beside the L hedge to the next road (250m). Continue on the track opposite winding down then up to the next road (1000m). ◇

④ Follow the road down R past a drive back R (350m) & on (150m).

⑤ Take the next R, in Dippenhall hamlet. Stay on the road down through the valley and up to the delta end (500m).

⑥ Enter the field opposite and converge to the R fence ¾ of the way down (200m). Cross several small fields ultimately aiming for the house at the far L corner. Exit between the garden fences to the tarmac drive (200m).

⑦ Walk down the drive and cross the main road into the entrance of Willey Mill (550m). Go R to the mill and through the garden on the path beside the house wall, crossing the River Wey. Disregard a footbridge to the island L and continue ahead over the relief channel (100m).

⑤ *Slightly shorter: Keep straight on over the grass to the next meadow (100m) and up under the railway (200m). Turn R.* ➔⑩

⑧ Turn L between river and pond and follow the river bank. When the river bends L (150m), continue R

around the field briefly (20m) then cross L to the adjacent field and carry on beside the river L (100m). At the edge of the flood plain climb the bank and follow the L edge of the field round to the track at the railway bridge (150m).

⑨ Pass under the railway and turn R up the footpath. Carry on beside the railway. Disregard the path L over the sandpit and one R under the railway (300m).

⑩ Keep on beside the railway past the sand pit (400m) and along the bottom of the fields to the next railway bridge (400m). ✳

⑪ Pass under the railway. At the bend in the track (50m) don't continue down to the footbridge but enter the meadow L and converge on the river. Carry on beside the river, through a wood and over several fences, to the next road at Bentley Mill (1000m). ☆

⑫ Cross the bridge and the dual carriageway to the *Bull* (150m).

The **Wey** starts as two rivers with the same name. The northern Wey rises west of Alton and is culverted under High Street in the valley. It flows past Bentley to Farnham and Waverley Abbey. The southern Wey starts as the Waggoner's Wells brooks and collects water from Selborne via the Oakhanger Stream and River Slea before flowing through Frensham. The confluence is at Tilford behind the *Barley Mow* and the main River Wey flows past the village green car park. After Elstead, Eashing and Godalming it cuts through the North Downs at Guildford, skirts Old Woking and joins the Thames at Weybridge. The name probably has the same derivation as *Wye* from an unknown Celtic word, perhaps descriptive, eg swift flowing.

12 Alice Holt Forest to Bentley

About 7 km/4¼ miles over the Wey valley; undulating; many stiles; very muddy in winter. The short cut of 2 km/1¼ miles and extension of 2 km/1¼ miles can be used together.   OS maps 1:25000 144 + 145, 1:50000 186 Aldershot.

Starting points: Alice Holt Forest, SU 802 433 (car park 100m from road on forest track at brow of hill), Bentley Station, SU 792 430 (free at weekends), Bentley village crossroads or near *The Bull*, SU 803 443, on the A31.

Linking walks   11☆ 13✽ ③1◇ ③3❖ ④1✲   **The Star** ☎ 01420 23184
The Bull ☎ 01420 22156
Millers ☎ 01420 22276

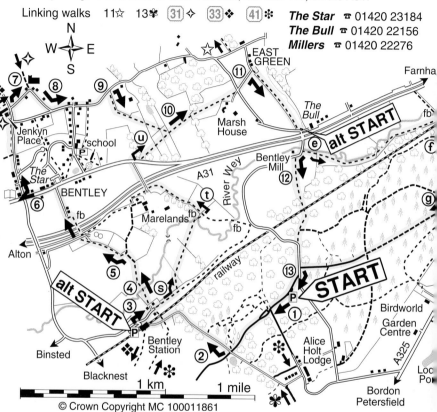

© Crown Copyright MC 100011861

✽① From the Alice Holt forest car park follow the track into the woods along the brow of the hill to the tarmac drive (700m).

② Walk down the tarmac drive R to Bentley Station (750m). ❖

③ Cross the railway and turn R along the road to the end (150m).

Ⓢ *Short cut of 2 km/1¼ miles missing the centre of Bentley: Continue along the field ahead (200m) then into the field L. Walk towards Marelands, the large house (100m), then bear R over the ditch. Keep on over the fields, diverging from the forest, to the river footbridge (200m downstream of the farm bridge) (350m). Cross.*

ⓣ *On the other side of the uphill hedge (40m) go L up the track and R over the A31 farm bridge (700m).*

ⓤ *Cross the road. Turn R (50m) then diverge from the road on the path over the fields (250m).* ➔⑩

④ Turn L between the houses. Follow the path down to the <u>River Wey</u> footbridge (150m) and up the other side to a R bend (300m).

⑤ Take the side path L along the R edge of the field, then R beside the sewage works fence (400m). Cross the footbridge over the dual carriageway A31and go up the lane emerging in the middle of <u>Bentley</u> near the ***Star*** (400m).

⑥ Go L on the main road to the cross roads (250m). See the Open Book beyond the Memorial Hall, then return and go up the minor road. Use the rising path on the L bank after the houses (600m). ◇

⑦ At Jenkyn Place turn R on the road to the church (300m).

⑧ From the church take the downhill road to the T-junction (250m) then L. Carry on past the R bend and Old Parsonage. Disregard the path R at the start of the field and continue to the path R at the end of the field (400m).

⑨ Turn off along the L edge of the field (150m). Continue around the bend L then across a corner to the next field and keep on in the same direction, obliquely down into the small valley and up to join another path at the hedge (400m). Turn L.

⑩ Carry on over the fields ultimately passing between the wood L and buildings R; take a line to the protruding corner of garden near the stables and go straight on to the drive (600m). Cross the road and continue on the lane ahead to the bend (200m). ☆

⑪ Turn R along the front of the first cottage and go through to the field. Follow the R edge (700m) then exit R to the road near the

Bull. Cross the dual carriageway and go along the minor road over the Wey near <u>Bentley Mill</u> (100m).

ⓔ *Extension of 2 km/1¼ miles: Enter the field L immediately after the bridge and stay near the river until the footbridge (1100m).*

ⓕ *From the top corner pass out under the railway and turn R. Diverge from the railway fence up the flank of the hill (100m) then go L on the track up through the trees to the level forest hard track on top (500m) (**Millers** pub 200m L). ❀*

ⓖ *Follow the main track R to the road (1200m). Go up L (40m). ➤⑬*

⑫ Disregard the footpath L at the bridge but soon after the river (50m) turn L at the next path in the field. Go straight up the field, through the wood and over the railway to the road (600m) then up L (200m).

⑬ Just over the brow go R on the forest track to the car park (100m).

Knopper galls develop as angular protruberences on acorns. Two or more together completely conceal the acorn. They are induced to grow when a 3mm relative of the wasps, *Andicus quercuscalicis*, lays its eggs on the acorns, providing food and housing for the larvæ. Some years the galls appear in great numbers.

These eggs have not been fertilized. The insects that emerge, mate and lay fertilized eggs on the male catkins of Turkey Oaks which induce small galls on the catkins. The females that emerge lay unfertilized eggs on acorns again, completing the cycle.

13 Alice Holt Forest and Rowledge

About 7½ km/4¾ miles around the central area of Alice Holt Forest with an extension of 2 km/1¼ mile along the River Wey; deciduous and conifer woods. OS maps 1:25000 145 Guildford, 1:50000 186 Aldershot.

Start at the forest car park near Rowledge Church, SU 820 430, or the one on the brow of the hill above Bentley Mill, SU 802 432, or pay to park at the Forest Centre, SU 811 417. On the extension, park beside the A31 near *The Bull*.

Linking walks   11✹   12❀   14✧   15✧   41✡

The Cherry Tree ☎ 01252 792105   **The Hare & Hounds** ☎ 01252 792287
Millers ☎ 01420 22276   **The Bull** ☎ 01420 22156
Forest Centre **Café** ☎ 01420 521267   **The Halfway House** ☎ 01420 22184

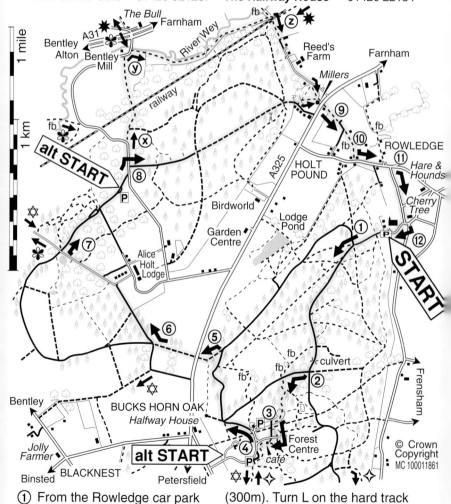

① From the Rowledge car park follow the track into Alice Holt Forest to the major track junction (300m). Turn L on the hard track and stay ahead to the valley with the culverted stream (900m). ✧

26

② Just up from the stream (80m), take the side track R to the first gravelled cross path (200m). Turn L up into the pines (100m) and fork R up to the car park (150m).

③ Halfway along the car park (150m) turn L on the gravel track to the Forest Centre (100m). Go R round the cabin *café* and over the grass to the pond (100m). ✿

④ Opposite the pond turn R on the branch drive past the entrance of the larger car park and continue along the hard track (300m). At the junction in the dip avoid the track ahead and ascend ½R. Stay on winding hard track up to the R bend where the track becomes almost straight and level (500m).

⑤ From the bend take the track back L round to the road (200m). Cross and go on along the track to the next cross track (300m). ✿

⑥ Go R on the hard track passing Alice Holt Lodge far R (500m). Bear L on the tarmac (450m). ❉

⑦ On the brow of the hill after the pond L, turn R either on the hard track or on the diverging path which curves round the arboretum back to the hard track (400m). Keep on to the road (300m).

ⓧ *Extension of 2 km/1¼ miles via the Wey: Go down the road L. At the L bend (250m) take the path ahead down through the wood, over the railway and down the field to the road (600m). Go R along the road briefly to the path R next to the River Wey bridge (50m).* ✱ *(The* **Bull** *is 150m further on.)*

ⓨ *Follow the path along the river through meadow and wood. Stay near the river until the path from the bridge across the river (1100m).*

ⓩ *From the top R corner go under the railway and straight up the path which becomes a track then tarmac (500m). Enter the 1st field R and cross ½L to the pub (100m).* ➡⑨

⑧ Down the road L (40m) take the track on the other side. Stay ahead over a major cross track (450m) and round the R curve to houses at Holt Pound (800m). Opposite the 1st house turn L into the field and aim ½R for the pub, **Millers** (100m).

⑨ Cross the pub garden and the road and follow the path opposite the pub. Stay ahead past the R bend in the cart track (250m) and down the footpath into the valley. Keep on up to the road (200m).

⑩ Walk up the road L (250m).

⑪ Turn R on School Road (400m) or go on to the **Hare & Hounds** (300m) then the 2nd R (400m).

⑫ Opposite the **Cherry Tree**, turn R along Church Lane to the forest car park (100m).

Forest in medieval times was a legal designation for areas set aside for the king's deer hunting. It was not necessarily woodland but included heaths and other uncultivated areas. Denizens had land to cultivate food but were not permitted fences, were allowed only crippled dogs and could not graze animals at fawning time. They incurred extreme penalties if they took game. Swainmote was the court for forest dwellers; their circuit judge was the Chief Justice of Eyre. Royal forests expanded until the 14th century when there were 68. It was possible to ride to the New Forest from Windsor without leaving forest. Forest law declined from the 16th century and was abandoned early in the 19th century when most of the royal forests were sold off.
The Law of Forestry W A Gordon HMSO 1955

14 Dockenfield and the sandpits

About 8 km/5miles; undulating forest and farmland; avoid in wet seasons; brambles in summer. OS maps 1:25000 145+133, 1:50000 186 Aldershot.

Start from the Abbotts Wood car park, SU 810 410, near Bucks Horn Oak.

Linking walks 13◇ 15★ 16❊ 41✦   **The Blue Bell** ☎ 01252 792801
The Halfway House ☎ 01420 22184
Forest Centre *Café* ☎ 01420 521267

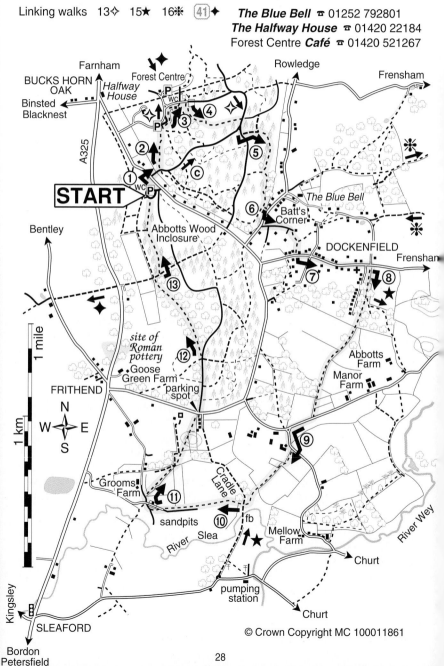

© Crown Copyright MC 100011861

① From the Abbotts Wood car park go out to the road and L along it (100m). Take the 1st track R to the path junction (100m).

ⓒ *Short cut of 400m: Keep on down the main track ahead to a T-junction (700m). Turn R.* ➧⑤

② Take the path L (300m). ✧

③ At the end turn R on the path round the pond to the cabin **café** then join the tarmac road (200m).

④ Just before the works gate take the path R and follow it down the valleyside (500m). At the track turn R to the fork (30m). Disregard the track R.

⑤ Cross the little valley (50m), and take the next L. When it bends L (100m), carry on ahead on the smaller winding path disregarding branch paths. Watch out for a house close by L just after a rise (700m). ✳

⑥ Just after the house take the path L to the road (30m). Go R briefly (100m) and down the first track L to houses (200m). At the end house diverge R down the footpath R across a valley and up between gardens to the road in Dockenfield (150m).

⑦ Follow the road L through Dockenfield, over the hill and down past the church (500m). ★

⑧ At the next side road R cross the grass diagonally to the footpath beside the field and carry on through the wood. Don't fork L near the end of the field L (200m) but go straight on to the end of the wood (200m) then continue ahead along the bottom L edges of the fields to the corner of the next wood (400m) and ahead along R edges to the road (200m).

⑨ Walk up the road R (200m) and take the side road L (150m). Just round the bend enter the first field R. Follow the R fence until it bends R (150m). Carry on in the same direction but L of the hedge down the fields (250m). In the bottom field cross slightly L round the flank of the hill to a stile concealed in the hedge (200m).

⑩ Cross the sunken track, Cradle Lane, and ascend the path on the other side. Over the top, follow the path past the sandpits to the front gate of the works (700m).

⑪ From the tarmac drive take the farm track R (40m) then turn into the 1st field R. Follow the diagonal footpath to the far L corner of the old hedge then to another (400m). After this keep on in the same oblique line over the hill to the furthest hedge corner beyond the houses R. The exit to the road is via a path R toward the last house but walkers tend to go out via the corner gate (300m). Cross the road and go up the forestry track (350m) (near the Roman pottery site).

⑫ Before the R curve, opposite the gravel side track bear L on the path through the scrub to its end near a field gate L (700m).

⑬ Turn R on the track away from the field (40m) then L up the first side track to the car park (500m).

The **Forestry Commission** was set up in 1919, after the First World War, for the strategic supply of timber. It has commercial and research divisions and provides policy, advice and grants. The commercial division, besides planting and logging, is responsible for access, including paths. The Commission has an open access policy on its own land.

15 Batt's Corner and the River Wey

About 9 km/5½ miles through Alice Holt forest and farmland; undulating; paths overgrown in summer. OS maps 1:25000 145 + 133, 1:50000 186 Aldershot.

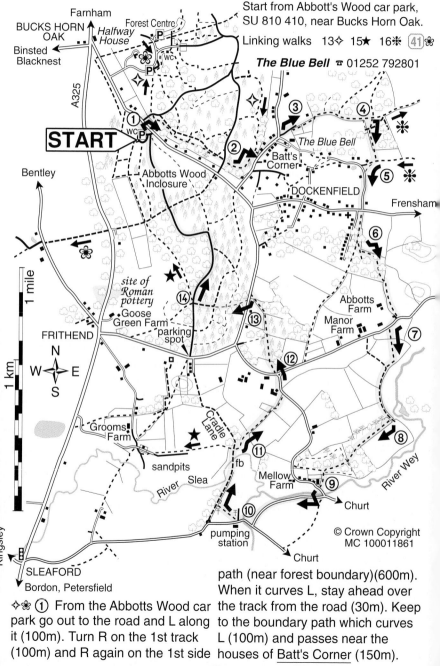

Start from Abbott's Wood car park, SU 810 410, near Bucks Horn Oak.

Linking walks   13◇ 15★ 16❋ 41❀

The Blue Bell ☎ 01252 792801

© Crown Copyright MC 100011861

◇❀ ① From the Abbotts Wood car park go out to the road and L along it (100m). Turn R on the 1st track (100m) and R again on the 1st side path (near forest boundary)(600m). When it curves L, stay ahead over the track from the road (30m). Keep to the boundary path which curves L (100m) and passes near the houses of Batt's Corner (150m).

② Watch out for houses through the trees R (with dog-walkers' paths) and exit via a path to the road. Carry on L along the road past the houses and the side road R with the **Blue Bell** (200m).

③ Just after this side road (10m), on the brow of the hill, turn R along the drive (100m) and join the path R of it. Keep to the L edge of the fields past the house (150m) and carry on in the wood beside the field. Ignore side paths L (350m). ✳

④ Just after the end of the field (50m) take the path down R, over the track from the field, to the bottom corner of the wood. Cross the field below (300m).

⑤ Outside, turn R then bear L on the side path down to the lane (100m). Follow the lane L to its end near Dockenfield Church (300m). Continue, over the road, along the hedge, through the little recreation field, into the wood (200m).

⑥ Before the end of the field L, branch L and go round the corner (50m). The path stays near the field (100m) then bends R through the wood to the furthest corner (200m). In the field turn R along the curving R edge to the road (250m).

⑦ Go R along the road (80m) then L across the fields in a straight line to the fence above the flood plain of the River Wey (250m). Turn R. Keep to the L edge through several fields round to the trees on the foot of the ridge rising R (400m).

⑧ 5m before the gate of the next field turn R on the path up the ridge through the trees to a high point (300m). Stay ahead gently down (250m). After the path steepens (50m) a side path drops L.

⑨ Either drop down the steps L and cross the small field to the road (100m) or stay ahead and go down the cliff steps (200m) then L down the road round past Mellow Farm (300m). Cross the bridge and walk along Smithy Lane R beside the River Wey (600m). At the T-junction turn R. Pass over the river and round the L bend (100m).

⑩ Just before the pumping station L, climb into the field R, in the corner between the road and the side track. Cross diagonally to the wood (150m) then follow the path R inside the edge of the wood (300m). Cross the River Slea footbridge and go on up to the side paths on both sides (70m). ★

⑪ Enter the field R. Swing L round the foot of the slope then cross to the gateway R (200m). Keep on up L of the hedge towards a house (250m). Go round the corner of the garden and on in the same direction at the L edge of the field to the road (200m).

⑫ Walk up the road L to the end (200m). From the L exit cross into the field and go up slightly diagonally L into the pine wood (70m). Carry on in the same line up the wood (400m), into the top field and on to the road L (50m).

⑬ Turn L on the road to the gate of Alice Holt Forest (Abbotts Wood) (40m). Go straight down the narrow path into the forest (200m). At the bottom stay ahead on the track to the major forest hard track (150m). The great Roman pottery was ¼ mile west of this point.

⑭ Turn R. Stay on this track round a L bend (100m) and R curve (200m) up to the car park (600m).

16 Frensham, Spreakley and Batt's Corner

About 9½ km/6 miles. A short cut of 1¼ km/¾ mile and an extension of 1¼ km/¾ mile can be used together. A good mix of wood, farmland and heath with views from two ridges. OS maps 1:25000 145+133; 1:50000 186 Aldershot.

Start from Frensham Great Pond car park, SU 843 406, or the recreation ground car park at Shortfield Common, SU 844 422.

Linking walks 14✳ 15✳ 17✿ 18✿

The Holly Bush ☎ 01252 793593
The Blue Bell ☎ 01252 792801
Frensham Pond Hotel ☎ 01252 795161

Frensham Heights

alt START Farnham Tilfor

The Holly Bush

SHORTFIELD COMMON

MILLBRIDGE

⑩

P

fb

⑨

⑪

Hall Place

SPREAKLEY

⑧

cart bridge

Woodhill Farm

⑦

fb

FRENSHAM

ridge

⑫

River Wey

Pitt Farm

⑤

⑥

Ⓢ

A287

The Blue Bell

Ⓧ

Batt's Corner

④

⑬

DOCKENFIELD

Dockenfield Farm

fb

Frensham Manor

START P

Frensham Great Pond

① From the car park make your way down to Frensham Great Pond. Follow the path R, along the edge to the road (500m).

② Walk down the road L to the first sluice (100m) and take the track R past a smaller pond to the River Wey (500m). Keep on near the river to Frensham Mill (800m).

③ Go L on the road, over the mill outlet, round to a junction (200m). Climb onto the verge opposite and go L (100m). At the house turn R on the path between fields up to the next house R (900m). ✳

①

②

Frensham Pond Hotel

Hindhead

© Crown Copyright MC 100011861

Ⓢ *Short cut of 1¼ km/¾ mile: Just before the house take the path R up the field into the corner of the wood (80m). Go up the edge of the wood (150m) then R on the track from the L field up to join the ridge path (100m).* ➔⑥

32

④ Stay ahead to the lane (100m) then R up to the end of the lane (250m). Carry on along the path to the next road (100m) and along that, forking R past the **Blue Bell** to the road junction (250m).

⑤ Turn R (10m) and R again along the drive (100m). Enter the field R. Keep to L edges past the house (150m) and stay ahead through the wood beside the field, disregarding side paths (500m).

⑥ Carry on along the ridge path out of the wood (100m) then at the R edge of fields (350m). After dropping a bit in the next wood (400m) enter the field R but keep on along the ridge (100m). Disregard side paths L & R. Go on through the next wood (150m) and round the edge of the field on the end of the ridge (250m). The distant large house L on the next hill is Frensham Heights.

⑦ Soon after the house behind the hedge, turn R out of the field. Stay ahead beside the L garden then down the drive to the road (150m). Go along the lane slightly R opposite (100m).

⑧ Take the first footpath L between fields and gardens up to the next road (300m).

⑨ Follow the road R up to Shortfield Common past the **Holly Bush** (250m) and on (100m).

⑩ Watch out for a path R into the recreation ground and cross to the middle of the bottom edge, skirting round the cricket pitch (250m).

⑪ From the path junction outside the field, take the path L, not the one next to the recreation ground but the other a few steps out, along the hedge above the little valley (200m). At the end of the bank join the cross path from the field L, and drop R to the stream (40m). ❀ Cross the culvert and follow the path along the R fence at the edge of the Wey flood plain (300m). Keep on round the R bend (overlooked by Rookery Farm and Old Vicarage) to the footbridge (300m).

⑫ Cross the river and follow the footpath which bends L (150m) up R of Frensham Church (250m) (or diverge R up through the churchyard R of the church). From the top end of the tarmac path, turn L on the road (40m), then R into Lovers Lane, the drive between gardens. Continue on the path, over a road with houses and up to the next road (400m). Sightly L (30m) take the heath path up the other side. Disregard the R fork and ascend to the cross path on the flat top of Frensham Common (150m).

ⓧ *Extension of 1¼ km/¾ mile: Slightly L, cross the level path and go straight down the hillside disregarding all side and cross paths (400m). Cross the road and go on up onto* King's Ridge *(400m).* ❀

ⓨ *See the view on the other side then go R along the ridge path to cluster of* barrows *(300m).*

ⓩ *Turn R on one of the footpaths between the barrows, down off the ridge to the road (400m). Cross to Great Pond and follow the edge R, round to the car park (500m).*

⑬ Go R on the level path (50m), round the curve and on down the hill, over several crossing paths to the pond (400m).

⑭ Turn R to the car park (200m).

17 Frensham, village and ponds

About 7½km/4½ miles; many variants possible; heathland relieved by ridges and ponds; confusing tracks and paths; good in winter; soft sand when dry. OS maps 1:25000 145+133, 1:50000 186 Aldershot.

Start from Priory Lane car park, SU 853 416, or from the National Trust car park at Frensham Great Pond, SU 843 406.

Linking walks 16✳ 18✳ 25✿ 29❖ 31★   ***The Bridge*** ☎ 01252 797360
Frensham Pond Hotel ☎ 01252 795161

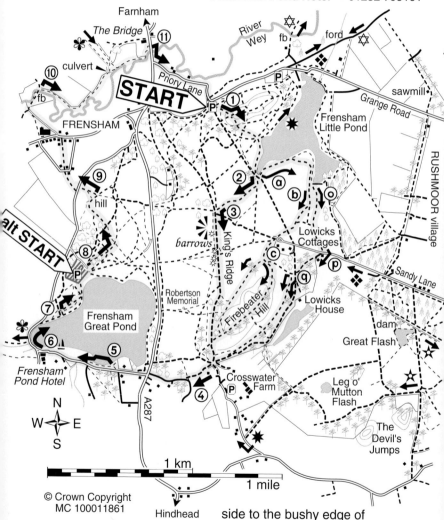

① From Priory Lane take the path diverging L from the car park up to steps (150m). At the top of the ridge, stay ahead down the other side to the bushy edge of Frensham Little Pond (300m). ✿✳❖ Turn R and follow the edge to the narrow end of the pond near the wide straight track (200m).

34

ⓐ *Alternatives: Keep to the path round the narrow end of the pond to the causeway at the end of the marshy creek L (600m). Don't cross the causeway but follow one of the two paths ahead:*
either ➔ⓞ *or* ➔ⓑ ☆
ⓞ *Take the L path ahead (500m).*
ⓟ *Cross the tarmac lane into the drive of Grey Walls and walk on along the track after it (250m).*
ⓠ *When another track joins from R either stay on the main track L along the boundary under trees or cross it and take the unshaded path low on the flank of Firebeater Hill, eventually re-joining the main track. Keep on to the 6-way track junction (800m).* ➔④
ⓑ *Take the R track ahead which curves R (150m), crosses a wide sandy track (200m) and passes the end of the tarmac at Lowicks Cottages (100m). Carry on ahead on the track outside the boundary R of the end cottage (150m).*
ⓒ *When the track curves L either continue on it round and up onto Firebeater Hill or take the path R round the flank ultimately bending L to re-join the main track on top. Keep on along the hill to the major crossing path (700m) and turn down L to the 6-way junction (100m). Bear R.* ➔④

② A wide sandy track passes the narrow end. Take the diverging path on the other side (70m) then fork R up to King's Ridge (300m).
③ Follow the ridge path L past the four barrows (300m) and keep on to the end of the ridge descending to the 6-way junction at the edge of Frensham Common (700m). Bear R onto the boundary track.

④ Follow the boundary track over the rises (200m) then join the track down R round the hill (250m). Cross the main road slightly L and carry on along Pond Lane (200m).
⑤ Just after the garden R bear R along the path near Frensham Great Pond, rejoining the road later (250m). Carry on ahead to **Frensham Pond Hotel** (250m).
⑥ At the junction go R on the road over the dam and sluices ✽ (50m). A little way on (100m) bear along the pondside path (150m).
⑦ Climb the stepped path and carry on above the pond to the car park (300m). Follow the outer edge diverging from the pond (200m).
⑧ At the corner of the ranger's hut furthest from the pond take the nearest path in the trees. Pass a cross path (120m) and bear L at the next side path (100m) up the slope. Cross the horse track (100m) and climb to the flat hilltop (80m). Keep on round the R curve to the cross path (150m).
⑨ Turn L down to the road (150m). Slightly L (30m) carry on down between fields, over one road and on to the next at Frensham (400m). Go L briefly (30m) then R down the tarmac path beside the churchyard (250m) and round the bend (200m).
⑩ Cross the River Wey and join the riverbank R. Follow the path along the fence of the flood plain meadow (300m), round the bend and on (300m). Cross the side stream and turn R. Keep to the footpath near the river to the road bridge below the **Bridge** (350m).
⑪ Go over the road bridge (100m) then L on Priory Lane and round the bend to the car park (550m).

18 Frensham Little Pond and the Devil's Jumps

About 8 km/5 miles with an extension of 2km/1½ mile; confusing heathland relieved by the hills and ponds; one steep hill; soft sand in summer; good in normal winters. OS maps 1:25000 145+133, 1:50000 186 Aldershot.

Start from the larger car park at Frensham Little Pond, SU 857 418 or from the road verge at the footpath near *The Pride of the Valley*, SU 870 393.

Linking walks   16✿   17✳   25✪   29✾   31★

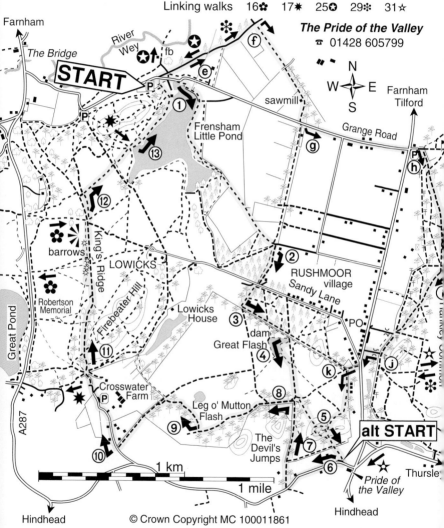

The Pride of the Valley
☎ 01428 605799

✪✾ⓔ *Extension of 2 km/1½ mile: From the bend in the road outside the car park follow the side track over the cross track (100m) and ford (250m) and on (400m).*

ⓕ *Take the bridleway R between fields to the next road (800m).*

ⓖ *Walk along the road L to the end (750m) and cross the main road into the lane ahead (60m).*

ⓗ *Take the forestry track R into Hankley Common (800m).*

ⓘ *At the 2nd downhill crossing track turn down R, not on the main track but the other diverging from it, which undulates and rejoins the main track (600m). Carry on beside the boundary (200m).*

ⓙ *At the 2nd side track R (opposite the summit of the hill L) exit to Rushmoor village (170m) and go L along the road (100m).*

ⓚ *Take the footpath R beside the end house at Sandy Lane to the 4-way path junction (100m) then go L up to the top of the hill - one of the* <u>Devil's Jumps</u> *(350m).* ➔⑤

① Follow the tarmac road round the end of the car park and past a creek (150m) then turn onto the path at the water's edge. After the dams (200m) stay on the path nearest the pond (600m). Ignore the side paths R after the end of the boggy area and keep straight on to the end at a track (400m).

② Turn R, not along the track but the path through the pinewood to the tarmac Sandy Lane (300m). Cross slightly R and go down the forestry track next to the gateway of Lowicks House (200m).

③ Carry on round the L bend, in- or outside the fence (400m). ☆

④ At the bottom, turn R on the crossing bridleway and R to Great Flash (pond). Follow the bank L of the pond (100m). Don't carry on R round the end of the pond but take the path ahead back to the bridleway (100m) and keep on over Frensham Common (250m). Cross the track at the foot of the hills (Devil's Jumps) and go up the steepest path (300m).

⑤ Notice where you arrive on top! Descend by the path on the S side of the hill. At the boundary keep on ahead on the fenced path to Jumps Road (300m). The **Pride of the Valley** is L (80m).

⑥ After the pub return to the path. Continue past it on the road (450m) (or return to Frensham Common (100m) and follow the boundary path L (300m).)

⑦ After the double curve in the road take the horse track down R beside the brook in the valley between two of the hills (600m).

⑧ After the last field L turn L along the boundary track of the common (300m). Keep on at the foot of the hills (400m).

⑨ Stay on the main track when it bends R. After L curves (300m) keep on to the road (500m).

⑩ Follow the road R past all the houses and Crosswater Farm (350m). At the end of the tarmac carry on up to the 6-way track junction at the edge of Frensham Common (150m). ✳

⑪ Cross the junction and take the R uphill path onto <u>King's Ridge</u> (500m). After the trees take to the L parallel path over the <u>barrows</u> ❖ (300m) then re-join the main ridge track at the isolated 4th barrow.

⑫ After this barrow (150m), paths descend L & R. Diverge on the path along the R edge of the ridge (100m) and turn down the first wide side path (250m). Cross the wide sandy track at the bottom and continue ahead until near the pond (250m).

⑬ Follow the path near water's edge which eventually bends L (450m) to the car park (200m).

19 Waverley Abbey and Crooksbury Hill

About 9 km/5½ miles; one steep hill; good for winter walking; fairly shady. An extension of 1 km/¾ mile to the *Shepherd & Flock* and a short cut of 2km/1½ miles can be used together. OS maps 1:25000 145 Guildford, 1:50000 186 Aldershot.

Start at Waverley Abbey car park, SU 870 455, or Crooksbury Hill car park, SU 878 457.

Linking walks   10☆   20✳   26✺

The Barley Mow at the Sands   ☎ 01252 782200
The Shepherd & Flock   ☎ 01252 716675

① Enter the field and follow the path. Pass between the Waverley Abbey ruins to the River Wey then return to the car park (700m).

② Walk out over the River Wey to the R bend (150m). From the side road go L between the houses to Mother Ludlam's Cave (150m). In wet seasons keep to the main path, ultimately through Moor Park courtyard (1300m). When dry, drop to the river, after the cave (150m). Follow the bank (400m) then turn R back to the main path at the pillbox (100m). Carry on (L) (800m).

③ At the road go L to the end (250m) then R (NDW) (150m).

④ At the bend take the footpath R (NDW) round the edge of the field and out to the track (400m).

ⓔ *Extension of 1 km/¾ mile via the* **Shepherd & Flock**: *Turn L and skirt the side of the valley (NDW). Disregard uphill paths L (500m).* ☆

ⓕ *Just under the railway, turn R through the garden of The Kiln (100m). Bear L over the footbridge to the road (150m). Cross the dual carriageway. Stay ahead towards* Bourne Mill, *but turn off through the subway to the pub (200m).*

ⓖ *Go down the lane at the side of the pub, under the road & railway (300m) and ahead (200m).* ➔⑥

⑤ Take the track R and pass over the footbridges to High Mill then out along the drive (400m). Turn R.

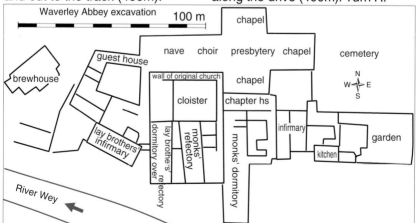

Waverley Abbey excavation   100 m

chapel · nave · choir · presbytery · chapel · cemetery · guest house · brewhouse · wall of original church · chapel · cloister · chapter hs · lay brothers infirmary · dormitory over · lay brothe's refectory · monks' refectory · monks' dormitory · infirmary · kitchen · garden · River Wey

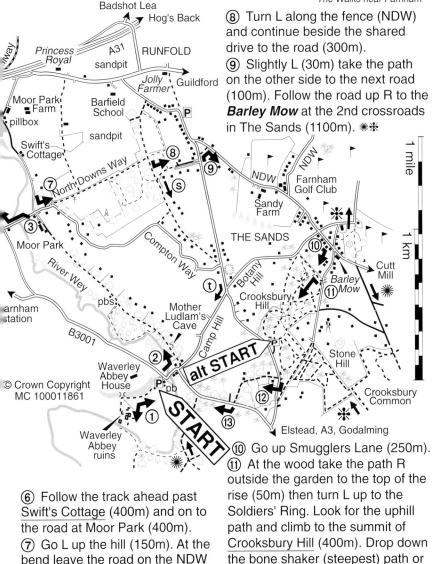

⑧ Turn L along the fence (NDW) and continue beside the shared drive to the road (300m).

⑨ Slightly L (30m) take the path on the other side to the next road (100m). Follow the road up R to the **Barley Mow** at the 2nd crossroads in The Sands (1100m). ❋❋

⑥ Follow the track ahead past Swift's Cottage (400m) and on to the road at Moor Park (400m).

⑦ Go L up the hill (150m). At the bend leave the road on the NDW footpath ahead along the edge of the field and into the wood (700m). At the end go R in the sunken track to the garden fence (150m).

ⓈShort cut of 2 km/1½ miles: Stay ahead on the path (700m). At the end follow the road R to the staggered crossroads (200m).

ⓣ Turn R down Camp Hill to the Abbey car park (600m).

⑩ Go up Smugglers Lane (250m).

⑪ At the wood take the path R outside the garden to the top of the rise (50m) then turn L up to the Soldiers' Ring. Look for the uphill path and climb to the summit of Crooksbury Hill (400m). Drop down the bone shaker (steepest) path or take the level path R and round down L (200m). Outside the end of the car park take the path down through the wood parallel with, then converging on the road (250m).

⑫ Cross the road towards the houses (Waverley Cottage) and go down the track to the end (500m).

⑬ Follow the road down R to the Abbey car park (600m).

20 Crooksbury Hill and Seale

About 9 km/5½ miles with a cut of 1½ km/1 mile: a North Downs Way walk; farmland, heath and woods; many shady parts; good in winter; confusing paths on Crooksbury Hill. OS maps 1:25000 145 Guildford, 1:50000 186 Aldershot.

Start from Binton Wood car park, SU 894 464, or Crooksbury Hill car park, SU 878 457, or Seale Church, SU 896 478 (roadside parking).

Linking walks 19✳ 21♣ 26✧

The Barley Mow ☎ 01252 782200
Seale Tea Room ☎ 01252 783661
Hog's Back Hotel ☎ 01252 782345

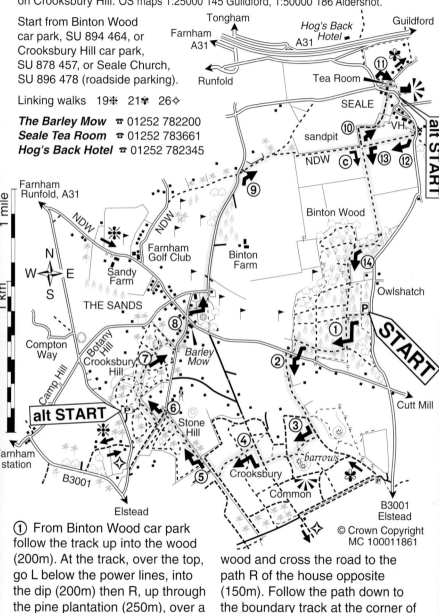

① From Binton Wood car park follow the track up into the wood (200m). At the track, over the top, go L below the power lines, into the dip (200m) then R, up through the pine plantation (250m), over a crossing track and on (150m).
② Just before a garden, find the small path L to the corner of the

wood and cross the road to the path R of the house opposite (150m). Follow the path down to the boundary track at the corner of Crooksbury Common (450m). Stay ahead, watching out for a side path up R (opposite a hilltop L) (150m)

③ Turn R up this narrow path over a hillock with bronze age barrows, L (200m). Cross a track and descend the heath path on the opposite side of the hill (200m). ✧
④ At the wide track go R (150m) then take the side path L to the W boundary of the Common (350m).
⑤ Follow the boundary track up R to the next corner (150m). Exit L but keep on in the same direction. Stay on the winding path just below the fence (400m). At the end go out from the top R corner to the end of the tarmac lane.
⑥ Turn L down the track which continues from the lane (100m). Take the first side path R uphill and stay below the gardens R (200m). At the R bend in the fence take the steep path L ever upwards to the top of Crooksbury Hill (150m). ✳
⑦ Leave the summit towards the Hog's Back (see directions on trig point). The path runs down a spur of the hill and branches to lanes on both sides. Make for the R lane by taking onward paths down this flank (350m). Walk down the lane (L) to the **Barley Mow** (300m).
⑧ Continue over the crossroads (50m) then take the path R between

gardens to the sports field. Cross slightly L to the exit (100m) and go L on the path past the house. Walk on along the lane past two drives of Binton Farm (800m).
⑨ After the S-bend, opposite the first house L, turn R on the North Downs Way (250m). Fork R and keep on to a track junction (700m).
ⓒ *Cut 1½ km/1 mile: Turn R.* ✦⑬
⑩ Go L on the cart track (100m), round the corner and on past barns down to Seale (350m). ❀
⑪ Go L on the road (50m) then R through Manor Farm craft centre (with **tea room**), to the path beyond (100m). Turn R to the church (50m). Re-join the road and turn L to the war memorial (100m) ↘ then R up the Elstead road (250m).
⑫ At the first field, just round the bend on top, take the footpath R (NDW) to the cross track at the end of the field (400m). Turn L.
⑬ Follow the track down the fields (600m) then up into Binton Wood (50m) soon swinging R (150m).
⑭ Go up round the L bend at the junction, into a dip beside a field L (250m) and over the top of the hill (200m) where the next track L leads to the car park (150m).

↘ The view from Seale War Memorial is along the dry valley below the Hogs Back. Gault clay allows the undermining of the chalk and malmstone to cause the steep escarpment. Malmstone is a calcareous sandstone seen in the white walls of the village. It constitutes the Upper Greensand along the North Downs.

The Folkstone Sands of the Lower Greensand emerging from beneath the Gault cause the rising ground covered by the heath of Puttenham Common, Crooksbury Hill and Frensham and Hankley Commons. The heathland used for army training above Normandy and Mytchett is on the sands of the Bagshot Series and flint gravel washed out of the chalk by Ice Age melt water.

21 Cutt Mill, Seale and Puttenham Common

About 9 km/5½ miles, with a short cut of 600m missing Seale. Heath, woods and farmland; shady; best when the heather is in flower but good in winter. The Puttenham Common paths are confusing; if lost make for the W boundary and follow it S to The Tarn. OS maps 1:25000 145 Guildford, 1:50000 186 Aldershot.

Start from Puttenham Common MIDDLE car park, SU 912 458, or Britty Wood car park, SU 904 456, or Seale Church, SU 896 478 (roadside parking).

Hog's Back Hotel ☎ 01252 782345   **Seale Tea Room** ☎ 01252 783661

Linking walks   20✿   22✱   23✿   26✪   ⟨1⟩✿   ⟨13⟩☆

Ramada Hog's Back Hotel

Hog's Back — Guildford
A31

pit

Tea Room

Downlands

⑨

A31 A331
ongham Farnham

⑧

Eastend

SEALE

alt START

unfold arnham

⑪ — Puttenham

Shoelands

⑦

NDW

⑩

North Downs Way

Ⓢ

✿✿ ✪☆

P

NDW

⑫

Binton Wood

⑥

Trout Pond

hillfort

ridge

⑤

brow

Owlshatch

P

Hampton Park

N W E S

1 mile

1 km

Long Pond

⑬

The Sands

General's Pond

④

Culvers

alt START

Warren Pond

②

①

P

P

Puttenham

⑭

barrows

P

③

Britty Wood

The Tarn
P

Cutt Mill Pond

START

Lower Common

Crooksbury Common

© Crown Copyright
MC 100011861
S Farnham B3001 Elstead

Elstead

Shackleford

42

(1) At the end of Middle car park take the main path away from the road into Puttenham Common (200m). Just after the marshy dip turn L on the side path to the Tarn. Follow the bank round R (150m) and cross the isthmus between the ponds (100m). At the corner of the Tarn turn L (20m) then R up the footpath past Warren Cottage (100m). Over the tarmac drive, go up the path near the R fence to a house R and cross the road to Britty Wood car park L (350m).

(2) From the car park entrance at the road, take the track into Britty Wood until level with the hill path L (200m). Fork R but soon (50m) diverge L onto the lesser path. Disregarding all side paths, carry on over the hill (250m) and down to the road (300m).

(3) Cross into the trees opposite and curve R to the track (80m). Turn L up to the gateway of Crooksbury Common (50m). ✿❦ Keep on up the R boundary track disregarding side tracks L (600m). When the boundary track bends ½L, branch off R on the path ahead and stay on it to the road (400m).

(4) Cross to the corner of the wood R of the house opposite, Gairholm. Follow the small path diverging from the garden fence to the wide track (100m). Turn R to the next track junction (150m). Go L over the hill and down (350m). When the track curves R take the smaller path L to stay near the edge of the wood. Watch out for the corner of the golf course L (200m).

(5) Soon after this (100m), turn away from the edge on the path across Binton Wood to the next track (250m). Up R (10m) carry on in the same direction (150m) and fork L, down to the field (50m).

(6) Go straight through the fields beside the hedge to the cross path, North Downs Way (600m).

(S) *Short cut of 600m: Go R on the NDW (400m), over the road and on to the tarmac drive & lodge (1500m) then L & R (70m). ➔(12)*

(7) Cross the NDW and go on up the cart track (100m), round R & L bends and down past barns to the road in Seale (350m).

(8) Turn R (50m) and L into the churchyard then L along the path past Manor Farm craft centre (with **Seale Tea Room**) to Wood Lane (70m). Walk up the lane past a footpath L (the best way to the **Hog's Back Hotel**) (150m), Seale chalkpit (100m) and ahead to the L bend at Downlands field (200m).

(9) Turn R down the path outside the field which zigzags around fields to a little wood. Skirt round the L edge of the wood down to the Puttenham road (700m).

(10) Walk along the road L (800m).

(11) Turn R on Totford Lane to the lodge (400m). Turn L (50m). ❀

(12) At the little car park turn R up the path into Puttenham Common (100m). Take the first side path R, but not the next R (100m). Keep on up over the ridge track (400m). Stay ahead over the brow of the hill (100m) and down into the dip with side paths L and R (250m). ✳✫

(13) Turn R on the side path over a slight rise. Keep on past an oblique cross path (300m) to a larger cross path in a little dip (120m).

(14) Turn R on this cross path (near the road) to the car park (300m).

22 Cutt Mill, Puttenham Common and Gatwick

About 6½ km/4 miles with an extension of 1½ km/1 mile; heath and wood; soft sand in summer. The heath paths are confusing. OS maps 1:25000 145 Guildford, 1:50000 186 Aldershot.

Start from Puttenham Common Top car park, SU 920 461, or Britty Wood car park, SU 904 455. Puttenham Common Lower car park beside The Tarn is close to the route, SU 909 457.

Linking walks
21✱ 23☆ 27★
⟨1⟩✱ ⟨13⟩✪

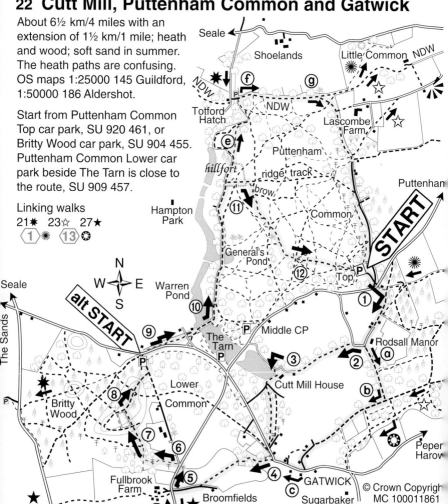

© Crown Copyright MC 100011861

1 km   1 mile

① From the Top car park of Puttenham Common, cross the road to the solitary house. Follow the path R of the garden and drop to the sunken track (200m). Walk down the track R and continue on the tarmac past Rodsall Manor House to the bend where there is a side path L (400m).

ⓐ *Alternative of equal length under trees to* Gatwick: *Follow the side path down then up to the T-junction in the wood (400m).* ✪

ⓑ *Turn R and keep going, disregarding all side paths. Just before the first house (650m) join the curving track ahead down to the road in Gatwick (150m).*

ⓒ *Walk along the road R (200m). After the stream (100m) at the bend just before the next house R take the path L.* ➔④

44

② Stay ahead up to the next path L (100m) and follow it though to another house (400m). Carry on along the drive and round the wall of Cutt Mill house (250m).

③ Just past the entrance turn off to the edge of the millpond and go L around the corner and along the dam (150m). At the end carry straight on across a cart track and follow the path through the heath (450m). Go L on the road (100m). Just after the galletted house take the path R from the bend.

④ Go through the trees, over a horse bridge into the field (200m). Follow the footpath across the field (in the slight depression) to the drive from the house (300m) and exit to the road (200m). ★

⑤ Turn R along the road to the next drive L (200m).

⑥ Don't follow the drive but enter the wood L. Walk through the trees parallel with the power lines to the 2nd pole (160m) and on beneath the cables.

⑦ Halfway to the 3rd pole (60m) look out for a path R and follow it into the wood (70m). Join a larger path up the hill through the larch plantation and over the top to the ridge path (250m). ✳

⑧ Follow the ridge path R, past several side paths to the other end of the ridge (200m) and carry on down to a wide track outside the edge of Britty Wood (150m). Turn L down the track through the car park to the road (100m).

⑨ Follow the road R. Watch out for a narrow path L (50m) and diverge from the road on it (300m). Cross the Hampton Park drive and go along the footpath R of the cottage drive to the Tarn (100m). Cross the dam between the Tarn and Warren Pond (100m) and go up the far bank (20m).

⑩ Turn L on the path up the W edge of Puttenham Common past General's Pond R (400m). Ignore side paths and continue up the steepening slope to the ridge path R in the hillfort just before the top (500m). In winter the Hampton Park house is visible below L. ✧✳

ⓔ *Extension of 1½ km/1 mile: Stay on the boundary path (200m) past a forking path L which rejoins later (200m), down to the T-junction (50m). Turn L (100m) and L again to the little car park at Totford Hatch on the* North Downs Way *(100m).*

ⓕ *Turn R up the NDW on the N boundary to the NE corner of the Common (600m).*

ⓖ *Before the corner cut across R (100m) and follow the E edge of the Common. The path becomes a track past two houses (550m). Soon after the second house join the parallel path in the trees R to the car park (800m).*

⑪ Turn R on the wide path and carry on up the ridge through the Iron Age hillfort (100m). Just after the exit notch in the ramparts (30m), bear R on the side path over the brow of the hill (100m) and down into the trees (200m). Disregard the cross path in the dip and go on over the rise to another cross path, sloping down R (300m).

⑫ Stay ahead on the rising wide path (not the one diverging R), over an oblique sunken valley path (300m) then up steeply to the Top car park (200m).

23 Puttenham Common and village

About 6½ km/4 miles with an extension of 1 km/¾ mile to Shackleford; good in winter; soft sand in summer. The route can be extended over Puttenham Common but the heath paths are very confusing. OS maps 1:25000 145 Guildford, 1:50000 186 Aldershot.

Start at Puttenham Common Top car park, SU 920 461, or at the roadside in the village, SU 930 478.

Linking walks 21❀ 22☆ 24❖
⟨2⟩❖ ⟨3⟩✳ ⟨6⟩✳ ⟨13⟩✩

The Good Intent ☎ 01483 810387
Jolly Farmer Harvester ☎ 01483 810374

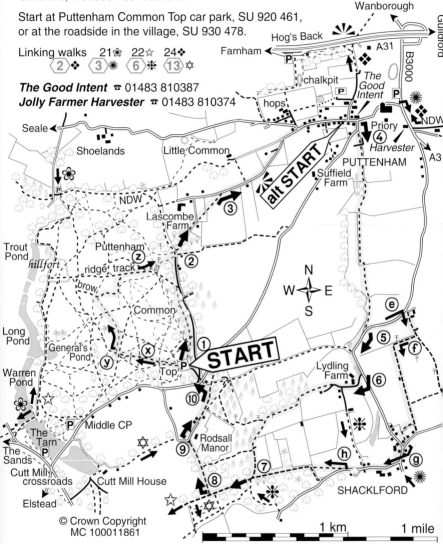

© Crown Copyright
MC 100011861

1 km   1 mile

❀ If new to Puttenham Common start at ① along the E boundary.   To see more of the Common, start at Ⓧ but allow time for confusion.

Ⓧ At the corner of the car park, furthest from the exit, descend the steep path (100m). Don't join the valley path but cross to the slight rise and keep on round the hillside, forking R when the path splits near the end, to the long straight sloping cross path (350m).

ⓨ *Turn R on the uphill path, not the main one but the lesser path diverging L from it, over a rise and down to a cross path below a hill (300m). Stay ahead up the steep slope (100m) then turn R along the brow of the hill (150m). Keep to the main path round the corner to the long straight ridge track (100m).*

ⓩ *Go R on the ridge track (200m). When it curves R, fork L on the path to the boundary track near a house (200m). Don't continue on the horse track ahead but take the woodland path slightly L (15m).* ➔ⓩ

① From Puttenham Common Top car park take the level path from the N corner into the trees and join the E boundary track R. Keep on past the two houses (800m). Just after the cottage disregard the bridleway R but turn into the wood R a few paces further on.

② Go straight through the wood and out to the drive of the house (300m). Cross the drive and a narrow field then the corner of the second field to the lane (300m).

③ Turn R on the lane and follow it down into Puttenham (600m). Continue through the village to the ***Good Intent*** L (600m). ✳❖

④ Opposite the pub, walk along Suffield Lane to the bend at the gate of Puttenham Priory L (70m) then take the footpath ahead along the L edge of the field, through a wooded part and on along the R edge of the next field (900m). Go L round the corner at the end (20m), then R into the next field and straight over to the stile hidden under the L brow at the dip (200m). Descend the short steep hill and keep R to the road (250m).

ⓔ *Extension of 1 km/¾ mile via* Shackleford: *Walk up the road L to the barns (300m). Turn R on the concrete track and immediately R along the soft track (150m).*

ⓕ *Turn R on the path along the hedge (150m) then L along the middle of the field (550m). At the hedge near the end turn R to the corner (100m) then L between gardens to the lane (80m)*

ⓖ *Turn R then L on the road through the village (150m). Take the side road R (250m). Disregard the footpath R after the last house and continue up the slope watching out for the side path up R (100m).*

ⓗ *Climb to the field and continue uphill diverging from the road to the middle of the top edge (200m). Join the track at the bend. Stay ahead passing a side track (400m).* ➔⑦

⑤ Go down the road R to the long roadside pond (300m).

⑥ After the pond turn R up the drive to Lydling Farm. Don't turn L at the side track (200m) ✳ but go on up past the drive of the last house. Stay on the track up round the winding edge of the wood to the 4-way track junction after the last field L (900m). Turn R.

⑦ Keep on down the sandy track in the wood (300m). ☆ ⚝

⑧ Turn R at the side track with a boundary mound R and continue to the lane (400m).

⑨ Turn R up the lane past Rodsall Manor. Keep on up the sunken bridleway under the trees, ignoring side paths R (350m).

⑩ Watch out for the side path L up the bank to a garden fence. Climb it and skirt the garden to the road opposite Top car park (150m).

24 Wanborough to Compton

About 8 km/5 miles; a scenic walk over fields; good all the year round; hilly; a crossing of the A31 dual carriageway and the hazards of golf.
OS maps 1:25000 145 Guildford, 1:50000 186 Aldershot.

Start at Wanborough Great Barn, SU 933 489 or the B3000 layby in Puttenham, SU 934 479, or at Watts Chapel in Compton, SU 956 474.

Linking walks 23 ❖ ①❖ ②♣ ③✳ ④✿ ⑤❋ ⑤❋ ⑱✦

The Harrow Inn ☎ 01483 810379   **The Good Intent** ☎ 01483 810387
Jolly Farmer Harvester ☎ 01483 810374   Watts Gallery ☎ 01483 810235
The Tea Shop at Watts' Gallery ☎ 01483 811030

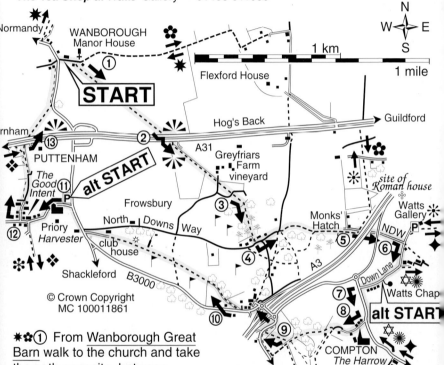

© Crown Copyright
MC 100011861

❋✿① From <u>Wanborough Great Barn</u> walk to the church and take the path opposite, between gardens, (old carriage way) up the <u>Hog's Back</u> (850m).

② Slightly L (30m), cross the dual carriageway to the stile and go down the L edge of the fields (450m). Cross the farm track & car park to the next field and take a line bisecting the corner (100m).

③ After the next track carry on ahead over the rough grass to the edge of a wood (100m) then ½R

down into the wood, over the golf course and beside a garden to the track (<u>North Downs Way</u>)(300m).

④ Turn L and disregard the R fork. Keep to the NDW (700m). ❋

⑤ At the end, follow the tarmac drive from <u>Monks' Hatch</u> under the bridges to the road (400m). ✦✿❋ (<u>Watts Gallery</u> and **Tea Shop** are 100m L from this junction.)

48

⑥ On the road go R past Coney-croft Farm (200m) to the cemetery (200m). Visit Watts Chapel in the cemetery then carry on to the end at the main road (200m).

⑦ Turn L. Follow the pavement down into Compton to Eastbury Lane R (250m). ✳ (The church and the *Harrow* are further on (300m).)

⑧ Walk along Eastbury Lane and continue on the bridleway (200m). Disregard the L fork and ascend. Watch out for a side path R on the brow of the hill (300m).

⑨ Take the path over the field and down to the road bend (200m). Follow the road down R, over the A3 bridge (300m) then L towards Puttenham (100m).

⑩ Turn R on the path next to the drive of Summer Wood. Continue round L behind the gardens to the path end then ahead through the the golf course (path obscure), L of Frowsbury (mound worth climbing) to the club house and road (1200m). Cross to the *Harvester* and go R up the pavement (100m).

⑪ Turn L down the side road, past Puttenham Priory and the church, into Puttenham (400m). ❖

⑫ After the *Good Intent*, turn R up School Lane and carry on when it becomes a track then bridleway. Fork R near the top (500m).

⑬ At the road walk along the verge R to the drive (20m) then cross the dual carriageway into the field opposite and descend diagonally R aiming for the point where the road below disappears under the hillside (300m). Walk down the path on the road verge L to Wanborough (200m).

The Domesday Book entry for Wanborough

The Domesday Book is on display in the National Archive at Kew. The text is relatively easy to read. Numbers are Roman. The first word is *Ipse*, himself, with a tall s. Words are shortened in a standard way: line 1 ten = *tenet*, holds; lines 1 & 3 tra = *terra*, land; lines 3 & 4 car = *carucatæ*, ploughs; line 4 dnio = *dominio*, demesne; line 6 TRE = *Tempore Regis Edwardi*, in the time of King Edward ie before the Conquest; lib, sol = *libra*, *solidos* as in £sd; *modo*, now.

In WOKING Hundred

Geoffrey himself holds WENEBERGE. It is not of the land of Asgar. Swein & Leofwin ^brothers^ held it from king Edward. Then it answered for 7 hides Now for 3 hides. ^Land^ for 7 ploughs. There were two manors; now it is one. In demesne is 1 plough; 12 villeins & 17 bordars with 8 ploughs. There is a church; 8 serfs. 6 acres of pasture. Woodland @ 30 pigs. Total value TRE £7; later 100 shillings; now £7.

25 Tilford, the Weys and Frensham Little Pond

About 7½ km/4¾ miles with extensions of 2¼ km/1½ miles and 1½ km/1 mile; a shady walk for summer mainly through woods and beside the Rivers Wey. OS maps 1:25000 145 Guildford, 1:50000 186 Aldershot.

Start at Tilford village green car park, SU 873 434, or the big car park at Frensham Little Pond, SU 857 418.

Linking walks 17✿ 18✪ 26✾ 27✸ 28✾ 29✪

The Barley Mow
01252 792205

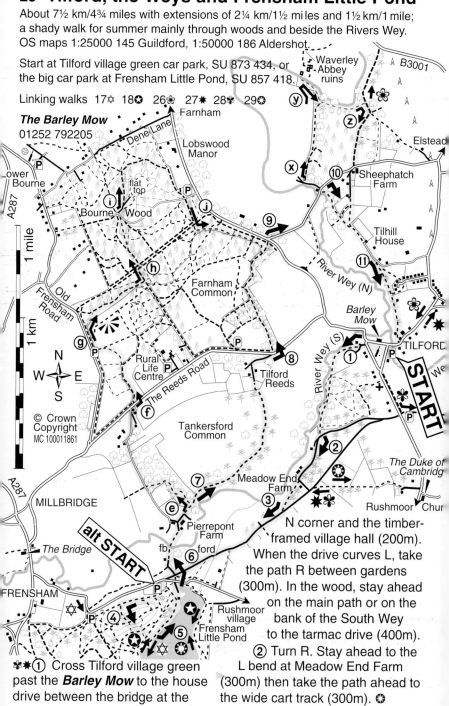

N corner and the timber-framed village hall (200m). When the drive curves L, take the path R between gardens (300m). In the wood, stay ahead on the main path or on the bank of the South Wey to the tarmac drive (400m).
②　Turn R. Stay ahead to the L bend at Meadow End Farm (300m) then take the path ahead to the wide cart track (300m). ✪

✾✸①　Cross Tilford village green past the **Barley Mow** to the house drive between the bridge at the

50

③ Keep on along the track, over the footbridge at the ford (550m) and past a cross track (300m) to the lane (100m).

④ Cross the car park away from the lane and walk along the path at the foot of the hill (300m) to the stepped path up L. Go over the ridge and down the other side to Frensham Little Pond (300m). ✿

⑤ Turn L along the edge of the pond (300m). ✪ At the house, go over the grass to the lane (100m). Cross the lane and go through the trees round L to the track (50m).

⑥ Cross the track and stay ahead on the lesser track to the next house (150m) then on the footpath over the South Wey to Pierrepont Farm (300m). After the timber barn turn R to the wood (100m).

ⓔ *Extension of 2¼ km/1½ miles: Take the side path L in the trees winding around the field (350m), eventually L to the farm drive (120m). Go R to the road (600m).*

ⓕ *Walk along the verge R (30m) then cross into the heath. Follow the track away from the road (300m). At R bend take the path ahead curving L to a wide path (200m). Keep on to the road (60m).*

ⓖ *Go up the bridleway beside the road past a path R (80m) to the corner of the fence R (80m) then climb R to the ridge track. Stay ahead to the cross track (500m)*

ⓗ *Drop L and cross both valley tracks (100m). Slightly R, go up the track (150m) and fork R up the 2nd bulge of the hill. Stay ahead to the L bend in the tarmac drive (250m).*

ⓘ *Don't go round the bend but turn R on the track which curves L (30m) then forks (50m). Descend L*

the flank of the hill. Avoid all L turns and keep to the main track down round the hill (Lobsworth Manor far L) to the tarmac drive (800m).

ⓙ *Stay ahead (200m). At the R bend cross the next track (20m) and take the path slightly R (40m). Turn L on the cross path. Follow it round the foot of the slope, bending R eventually to a Y-junction (500m). Descend L to the road (100m). ➜⑨*

⑦ Stay ahead through woods and heath to the next houses (1400m).

⑧ At the T-junction of tracks turn R up to the road (200m). Cross to the track opposite and carry on through to the main road (850m).

⑨ Follow the minor road opposite and cross the North Wey at Tilford Mill Bridge (500m). ❀

ⓧ *Extension of 1½ km/1 mile: After the house go L on the track to the fields (150m) then R up the path in the edge of the wood (500m).*

ⓨ *At the river go L to see the Waverley Abbey ruins on the other side (200m) then return and keep on above the river (400m).*

ⓩ *At the track, turn R to the 4-way junction (100m) then R again up to the lane (400m). Continue ahead on the track opposite which becomes a descending path then a tarmac drive (600m). ➜⑪*

⑩ Immediately after the river turn off the road up the path R. When another path joins from the L (300m) continue ahead (150m) and along the the tarmac drive (200m).

⑪ At the L bend after Tilhill House bear R on the bridleway down to the road in Tilford (passing a pillbox and the Wey confluence R)(500m). Turn R and cross the Tilford Bridge (main Wey) to the green (100m).

26 Tilford, The Sands and Crooksbury Hill

About 9½ km/5¾ miles over farmland and heath; one very steep but avoidable hill; soft sand in summer; fairly shady; good in winter. OS maps 1:25000 145 Guildford, 1:50000 186 Aldershot.

Start at Tilford village green car park, SU 873 434, or Crooksbury Hill car park, SU 878 457.

Linking walks 19✳ 20◇ 21✪ 25✿ 27❖ 28❄

The Barley Mow at The Sands ☎ 01252 782200
The Barley Mow at Tilford ☎ 01252 792205
The Donkey ☎ 01252 702124

NDW

Binton Farm

N
W E
S

Aldershot A31
Runfold

THE SANDS

Compton Way

Botany Hill

Crooksbury Hill

Barley Mow

Cutt Mill

Camp Hill

cave

Farnham station
B3001

Waverley Abbey House

Stone Hill

Crooksbury Common

alt START

Waverley Abbey ruins

Sheephatch Farm

1 km

1 mile

B3001

Elstead

Tilhill House

The Donkey

River Wey (N)

Farnham station

Barley Mow

River Wey

TILFORD

Millbridge Frensham

Whitmead

© Crown Copyright
MC 100011861

River Wey (S)

VH
wc

START

Churt Hindhead

52

✤①　From Tilford green cross the bridge between the car park and the **Barley Mow** (100m). Almost immediately turn L on the footpath. See the Wey confluence L just after the pillbox (100m) and carry on (400m). Continue along the tarmac drive past Tilhill House to the end (200m) and ahead into the wood (200m).

②　When the path forks, take the R branch and keep on up to the road at Sheephatch Farm (400m).

③　Cross the road and go down the forestry track to the T-junction (350m) then L to the next road. The ruins of Waverley Abbey are visible far L (500m). ✳

④　Walk up the road R (250m).

⑤　Go up the track L just after the gateway of Keeper's Cottage (500m) and cross the next road to the footpath in the trees.

⑥　Turn L. Follow paths diverging slightly from the road up to the car park (200m) and climb one of the steep paths to the summit of Crooksbury Hill (200m). See the directions on the trig point.

Ⓢ *Slightly shorter route: Descend towards Gibbet Hill (50m). Aim for the garden corner and follow the winding path below (R of) the fence, around the hill (200m). At the uphill track turn L up the start of the tarmac lane (100m) then turn R into the wood and keep to the zigzag path below the fence around the hillside (400m).*

Ⓣ *At the end, exit to Crooksbury Common but go on in the same direction down the boundary track R (200m). Take the path L across the heath to the wide track (350m) Turn R.* ➤⑨

⑦　Leave the trig point towards the Hog's Back. The path runs down a spur of the hill branching to lanes on both sides. Make for the R lane Smugglers Way via onward paths down the R flank (400m). Go down the lane L to the **Barley Mow** in The Sands (200m). ✧❂

⑧　Go R at the crossroads (200m) and take the 1st R (Long Hill), the straight ascending track (350m). Stay ahead over the ridge and into Crooksbury Common (450m).

⑨　Keep to the wide sandy track to the boundary (550m) and on past the houses and through the former Charles Hill estate down to the road near the **Donkey** (800m). ❖

⑩　Go down past the pub and up to the track junction at the end of the tarmac (200m). Go L past a large house and on along the path to the road at Whitmead (1200m).

⑪　Follow the uphill road R to the 1st house L, Pooh Corner (300m).

⑫　Turn L into the house drive and go on between fields and along the tarmac drive to the end (650m).

⑬　Turn L & R to the parallel lane and go on to the main road then L down through Tilford, over the Wey to the village green (600m). ✳

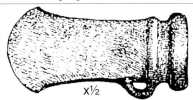

x½

Bronze axe head of the late Bronze Age, perhaps 900BC, found 4 feet down, during the digging of a soak-away at a house on the east side of Smugglers Way, The Sands.

Surrey Archæological Collections Vol 55 1958 courtesy of Surrey Archæological Society

27 Tilford to Elstead

About 9½ km/6 miles with small extensions of 600m and 800m but no short cuts; through heath and farmland; not much shade; soft sand in summer; a good winter walk. OS maps 1:25000 145 Guildford, 1:50000 186 Aldershot.

Start at Tilford Green car park, SU 873 434, or in Elstead, SU 905 435 (park in the Thursley Road layby between the green and the church).

Linking walks   22★ 25✴ 26❖ 28☆ ⟨13⟩ ♣ ⟨14⟩ ✿

The Barley Mow at Tilford ☎ 01252 792205
Duke of Cambridge ☎ 01252 792236
The Donkey ☎ 01252 702124
The Golden Fleece ☎ 01252 702349
The Woolpack ☎ 01252 703106
Elstead Mill ☎ 01252 703333

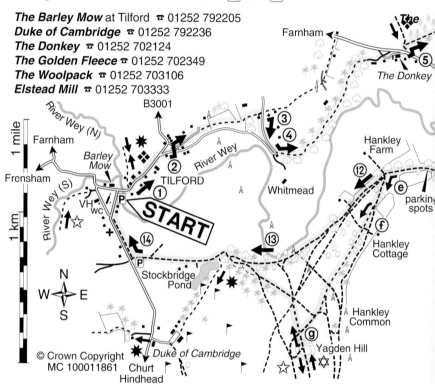

❖① From the green at Tilford, cross the east bridge, between the car park and the **Barley Mow** and continue beside the road (450m).

② Turn R along Whitmead Lane (100m) then L and immediately R on the shared tarmac drive (200m). At the end carry on along the footpath between fields and out L of the house to the road (400m).

③ Don't continue on the path opposite but go down the road R to Whitmead Lodge (300m).

④ From the hairpin bend take the byway L to the first house (1000m). At the next junction (100m) go R down the tarmac lane past the **Donkey** and up to the road (200m).

> *The Donkey* claims to be the only pub of that name. Licensed in 1850 as the *Halfway House*, it was nicknamed the *Donkey*, because, until around 1900, the landlord kept six donkeys for hire to help carters get their waggons up the hill. It changed its name in 1947.

⑤ Go up the cart track opposite. then turn R uphill on the sandy bridleway (300m). At the tarmac drive keep on ahead to the gates of Three Barrows Place and out L over the road (300m).

⑥ Continue ahead between the fields, emerging on the next road beside Fullbrook Farm (750m). ❀❀★

⑦ Go R down the road round R and L curves (600m).

⑧ Join the footpath L at the first cottage. Behind the garden turn L along the fence then stay on the footpath beside the River Wey to the main road at Elstead (650m).

⑨ Cross into the drive to see **Elstead Mill** then go back along the road, over Elstead Bridge and up past the **Golden Fleece** to the village green (300m). ✿

ⓧ *Extension of 600m: Carry on ahead past the **Woolpack** to the next side road R (300m).*

ⓨ *Turn R into Springfield then R into Back Lane and L after the 1st house. Continue upwards to the path junction on the hilltop (350m).*

ⓩ *Go down the footpath almost ahead, round the outside of the field, then down the road to the church (300m).* ➔⑪

⑩ Turn R past the shops and R along the Thursley road (400m).

⑪ From Elstead Church follow the side lane (Westbrook Hill) to the brook (from the Devil's Punch Bowl) (350m) and past Westbrook Farm R and the house, Westbrook, L. When the tarmac ends (550m) fork R along the broad vehicle track to the 4-way junction in the corner of Hankley Common (Hankley Farm, R) (400m).

ⓔ *Extension of 800m/½ mile over Yagden Hill: Turn L on the E boundary track (200m).*

ⓕ *Where the track is deflected by the corner of the field, diverge R on the lesser track. Pass under power cables (600m) and follow upward paths to the top of Yagden Hill (500m).* ☆

ⓖ *Return down the N side, towards the distant Crooksbury Hill telecommunications mast (3½ km away) and carry on in the same direction to the boundary track above a bend in the River Wey (550m). Turn L.* ➔⑬

⑫ Keep on ahead along the N boundary track, disregarding all side tracks. Pass a house down R (300m), power cables (450m), and a bend in the river R (200m).

⑬ Continue on the boundary track, round R & L bends (450m) to Stockbridge Pond ✳ and ahead to the road (550m).

⑭ Turn R on the bridleway beside the road to the green at Tilford. Bear R to the car park (400m).

28 Tilford to the Lion's Mouth

About 7 km/4½ miles with a short cut of 3 km/2 miles; mainly over heath; good in winter; soft sand in summer. Hankley Common is owned by the army but open to walkers; rarely you may find yourself in the middle of an army exercise. OS maps 1:25000 145 Guildford, 1:50000 186 Aldershot.

Start from the village green car park at Tilford, SU 873 434.

Linking walks   25 ❀   26 ❀   27 ☆   29 ◇   30 ✳   31 ✳   ⟨14⟩ ✦

Barley Mow, Tilford ☎ 01252 792205   **Duke of Cambridge** ☎ 01252 792236

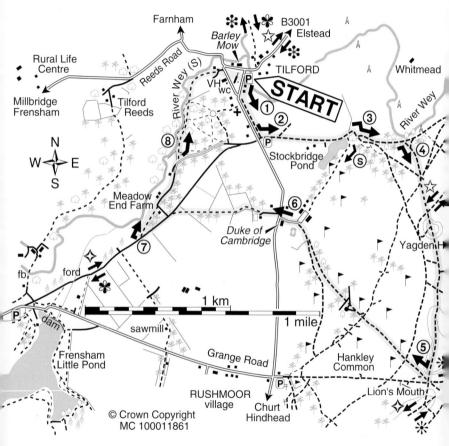

☆① At Tilford green make for the corner furthest from the **Barley Mow** (150m) and go on along the bridleway L of the road (300m).

② Take the track L to the far end of Stockbridge Pond (600m).

Ⓢ *Short cut of 3km/2 miles: Turn R on the path across the end of* the pond. Stay on it all the way to the golf club car park (600m) . ✦⑥

③ Continue on the main track round R & L bends into Hankley Common (100m) and take the L track at the fork. Stay on this track until the River Wey is just below it L (300m).

④ Turn R on the side track up to the 6-way junction (300m) and go on ever upwards to the top of Yagden Hill (300m). ✦ Continue on the same track beyond the hill, rising again along the ridge to the Lion's Mouth (a cleft) (1000m). ✧❋

⑤ Drop into the cleft and descend from the ridge by the first track R. Keep on in the same line all the way to the road. After the 1st cross track (200m) the route is through the golf course. After the 2nd cross track (450m) disregard the R fork. Eventually join the track converging from L (650m) and go on past the club house and car park (150m).

⑥ Follow the tarmac drive up to the **Duke of Cambridge** (120m). Over the road slightly R (30m) walk up the drive to Markham (150m).

At the gate take the path that skirts R of the garden and carry on between the fields to the end (600m). Bear L along the track past the gateway of Meadow End Farm to the side path back R between fences (300m). ❦

⑦ Follow this path to the farm (250m) and carry on along the drive past the houses (350m).

⑧ Just after the last small field turn off on the footpath L through the trees to the River Wey S and go on beside it. The lesser path on the river bank offers better views but needs caution (500m). Eventually pass through the gate into the garden and keep on ahead to the road (300m). Cross the cricket green to the car park beside the River Wey (150m). ❋

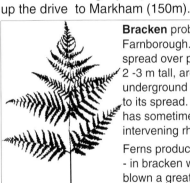

Bracken probably provided the *farn* in Farnham and Farnborough. It is a typical fern except in its ability to spread over poor, dry soils. The fronds, which may be 2 -3 m tall, are single leaves thrust up from a creeping underground stem. It is this rhizome which is the key to its spread. DNA analysis shows the same individual has sometimes spread over a mile or two, though the intervening rhizome may have disappeared.

Ferns produce spores on the underside of their leaves - in bracken within the rolled edges. A spore may be blown a great distance but it does not develop into the same type of plant as its parent. It forms an obscure filmy plant about 8mm across without stems or leaves which can survive only on wet soil in high humidity. This reproduces sexually. The offspring develop into the familiar fern plants but *in situ* in the damp places of their parents. The rhizome has enabled bracken to side-step this limitation.

Besides tolerating poor ground, bracken poisons the soil against other plants and deters animals from eating it. Leaf nectaries feed ants which defend it. A thiamine-destroying enzyme in the fronds causes vitamin deficiency in horses and pigs and an unknown agent causes haemorrhaging in ruminants. The rhizome allows it to stockpile scarce nutrients and withstand heath fires.

Because of its resistant wind-borne spores, bracken travels far and wide. It is cosmopolitan wherever the climate is temperate, though splitter botanists elevate the local varieties to sub-species or species. A population explosion of bracken is occurring in tropical highlands where forests have been cleared.

29 Frensham Little Pond and the Lion's Mouth

About 10 km/6 miles with an extension of 1 km/¾ mile to Devil's Jumps; mainly heath; short steep hills; good in winter. Hankley Common belongs to the army but is open to walkers. OS maps 1:25000 145+133, 1:50000 186 Aldershot.

Start from Frensham Little Pond car park, SU 857 418. Other parking spots: near the *Duke of Cambridge*, SU 876 424; on the roadside in Rushmoor, SU 872 401, and at the footpath up from the *Pride of the Valley*, SU 871 393.

Linking walks 17❖ 18❇ 25◉ 28◇ 30✿ 31❇ 32☀

Duke of Cambridge ☎ 01252 792236   **Pride of the Valley** ☎ 01428 605799

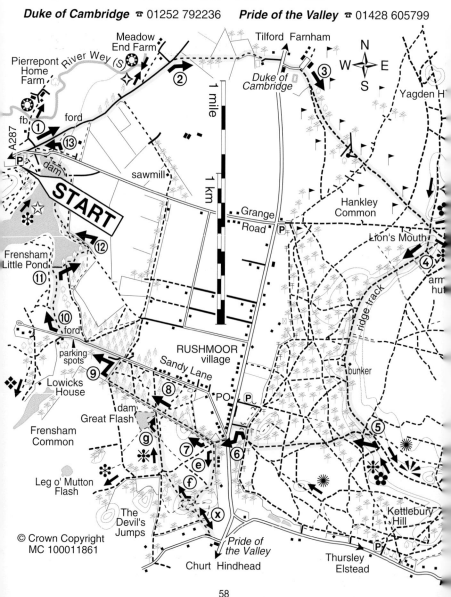

© Crown Copyright
MC 100011861

① Take the cart track from the bend in the lane outside Frensham Little Pond car park. Pass the side track L (100m) ✿, ford (300m), side path L (550m) ✧ and gateway of Meadow End Farm L (200m).

② Just after this (30m) bear R on the footpath R between the fields. Eventually this skirts a garden and joins a house drive (600m). Keep on down to the main road (150m) and cross to the pub (30m).

③ Walk down the tarmac drive beside the **Duke of Cambridge** (120m). At the golf club car park follow the sandy cart track curving R into Hankley Common (150m). At the corner of the field R, fork L on the bridleway. Disregard cross and side tracks (1100m) and keep going from the top of the golf links up to the Lion's Mouth, a sandy cleft in the ridge (200m). ✿✳

④ Climb the 1st side path R onto the ridge R. Stay on the ridge track past a little concrete army bunker L (1200m) and on round a slight R curve (300m) to two oblique cross tracks 50m apart (150m). ✳

⑤ At the 2nd crossing track (with boundary stone) turn back R off the ridge. Cross the other track from the ridge and go on down crossing several more tracks. Just over the next rise (450m) fork R. After the next cross track (200m) keep on over the foot of the hill and down to the boundary (300m).

⑥ Turn R (70m) then L to the road in Rushmoor village (170m). Cross to the pavement and follow the road L to Sandy Lane (100m). Take the path next to the end house to the 4-way junction on Frensham Common (100m). ✳

ⓔ *Extension of 1 km/¾ mile to the Devil's Jumps: Take the path L (150m). After the houses, diverge from the boundary up onto a col (300m) then R to the top (70m).*

ⓧ *For the **Pride of the Valley**, continue ahead from the col down to the road (300m) and L to the pub (80m) then return to the top.*

ⓕ *From the top drop down the path on the north side towards the largest pond - Great Flash. Cross the junction at the foot (300m) and take the track ahead until paths diverge on both sides (250m).*

ⓖ *Diverge L to the pond (100m) then R along the water's edge back to the track at the boundary of Frensham Common (150m). Go L beside the fence, inside or out.* ➔⑧

⑦ Turn R along the fence either on the footpath in the Common or the track outside. Go over a hillock and down over the cross track near the pond, Great Flash (500m).

⑧ Stay beside the boundary until the main track bends R (350m).

⑨ Go round the bend to Sandy Lane (200m). Follow it L (400m). ✧

⑩ Just after the footbridge at the ford (50m), opposite the drive of Grey Walls L, take the path R. Disregard side tracks (500m).

⑪ When another track converges L to run alongside turn R along the causeway (100m) then follow the winding path L to the Common boundary (200m).

⑫ Turn L and keep to paths at the edge of Frensham Little Pond all the way to the stone dam (650m). Keep on beside it until the water's edge meets the road (200m).

⑬ Follow the lane L (100m) and cross L to the car park (200m).

30 Thursley and Hankley Commons

About 9 km/5½ miles; allow time for confusion; best when the heather is in flower; splendid open heath; short steep inclines; little shade, stony and soft sandy tracks. OS maps 1:50000 145+133, 1:50000 186 Aldershot.

Start at The Moat car park, SU 899 416, or at Thursley recreation ground, SU 899 398; park on the grass near the children's play area.

Linking walks 28✳ 29✿ 31✛ 32☆ ⟨14⟩✳ ⟨15⟩★ ⟨16⟩✪ ⟨18⟩❖ ⟨19⟩◈ ⟨20⟩☆

The Three Horseshoes ☎ 01252 703268

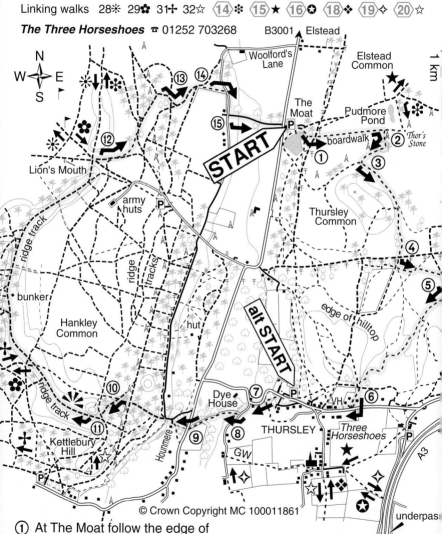

© Crown Copyright MC 100011861

① At The Moat follow the edge of the pond away from the road past the 1st marshy corner (150m) and turn L on one of the paths to the wide sandy track with electricity poles (50m). Continue on the footpath on the other side which is Thursley Common Nature Trail. It is opposite one of the paths from the pond but if you choose the wrong one, hunt for the onward

60

footpath. It soon becomes board-walks along an ancient boundary mound through the bog (500m). ★

② Just before Pudmore Pond L, turn off R, past a pylon into the clump of trees on hard ground (100m) then curve R. Keep on to the edge of the hill (200m).

③ Turn L on the path which skirts the base of the hill. Disregard the path R over the hill (400m) and keep on (400m). Cross the wide sandy track and continue ahead to the 4-way junction near the corner of a disused field (70m).

④ Go L, round an S bend to the broad sandy track (350m). Turn R along this wide track (100m). ❂❖

⑤ Just before the L bend turn R on the path to the cleft in the hillside (300m). Keep on up the steep escarpment and across the flat top, winding to the broad boundary track (700m).

⑥ Cross it and follow the track, opposite, between gardens into Thursley (200m). Go R down the road past the **Three Horseshoes** and Street House (300m) ☆◇ to the recreation ground (150m).

⑦ Opposite the cricket field track diverge L on the path under the trees down into the valley (200m) and go on down the road (100m).

⑧ Before the bridge turn L up the lane (100m). Just after the Dye House above R, turn off R up the edge of the field and go on up the valley side, over the Dye House stream and on to the road (400m).

⑨ Cross and go straight down the steep (unofficial) path to Hounmere house (100m). Walk down the drive and round L over the brook (70m). Don't follow the R bend but take the branch track ahead (300m). Cross the track with the pylons and go straight on through the pines (no path) to the next track (100m).

⑩ Ascend L to the track junction on the ridge top (200m). ✛

⑪ Turn R. Climb the little knoll for the view then go on along the ridge track past two oblique crossing paths (600m), ✿ a little bunker R (450m) and ahead (1000m). Just before the end, diverge L down the flank into the Lion's Mouth, a cleft in the ridge (200m). ✾✴

⑫ Turn R. Two tracks descend. Start down the L one (150m) then diverge on the side track L round the foot of the hill to cut a corner (200m). Carry on along the next broad track. Disregard the tracks forking up L and pass under the electricity cables (250m) to the next major junction (100m).

⑬ Turn R down past side tracks L & R to the T-junction (200m) then L to the junction with the converging boundary track (200m).

⑭ Cross to the fence corner R in the trees. Follow the fence to the lane (300m) then go R (150m).

⑮ Opposite the gate of Elstead Manor turn L on the track to the road opposite The Moat (400m).

The heath lichen *Cladonia pomentosa* (= *C. impexa*), small portion, actual size. It flourishes in winter and looks like wads of greenish cotton wool on heather just above the ground. Lichen should be pronounced *liken*. Each species is a compound organism consisting of a filamentous photosynthetic bacterium (formerly classified as a blue-green alga) and a fungus.

31 The Hankley Common ridges

About 8 km/5 miles over heath ridges with short steep hills; confusing tracks and paths; good in winter. OS maps 1:25000 145+133, 1:50000 186 Aldershot.

Park at Hankley Common car park, SU 891 411 (up a long tarmac drive from the S-bend in the Elstead-Thursley road) or on the roadside at the path near the *Pride of the Valley*, SU 871 393.

Linking 17★ 18★ 28✳ 29✳ 30✛ 32✳ *Pride of the Valley* ☎ 01428 605799

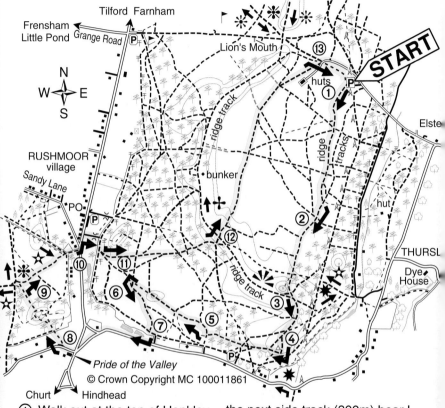

Tilford Farnham

Frensham
Little Pond Grange Road

Lion's Mouth

huts

START

Elste

N
W E
S

RUSHMOOR
village

Sandy Lane

bunker

ridge track

ridge tracks

hut

THURSL

Dye
House

PO

ridge track

Pride of the Valley

© Crown Copyright MC 100011861

Churt   Hindhead

① Walk out at the top of Hankley Common car park and follow the ridge path L (800m).

② Drop off the end of the ridge and stay ahead up to the track junction on the high ridge (700m). Climb the little knoll back R for the view northwards then return to the junction (200m). ✳

③ Continue ahead, not along the ridge. After an oblique cross path the track rises on Kettlebury Hill. At

the next side track (300m) bear L up to the trig point (100m).

④ Follow the ridge R down past many side paths and up again.

⑤ At the cross path on the end of the ridge (500m) don't go on but descend R (100m) then turn L in the original direction. Carry on over the next ironstone hill (350m).

⑥ After the top (80m or 200m) take one of the tracks L down the hillside to the boundary (400m).

⑦ Go out to the road (100m) and down R. Don't fork R (650m). Over the main road go on past the front of the **Pride of the Valley** (80m).

⑧ At the slight L bend take the footpath R ever upwards to the top of the Devil's Jump (300m). Go round the ironstone crown and descend by the path on the N side ie towards the pond (250m). ✳

⑨ At the foot of the hill take the R path up to the corner of Frensham Common (400m) and on down to the road in Rushmoor (100m).

⑩ Walk along the main road L (100m) and take the track R in the trees to Hankley Common (150m).

⑪ Turn R on the boundary track but soon (70m) diverge L on the track skirting nearest the hill. Stay on this track, disregarding several cross tracks, until it rises onto the next major ridge (800m). ✛

⑫ Just before the top of the ridge turn L on the crossing path L to the top (40m). Pass over the ridge track obliquely and follow the onward path down the flank of the ridge then along the bottom of the basin to the army huts (1200m). ✳

⑬ After the huts either take one of the steep paths up R to the car park on the ridge above (300m) or go up the tarmac road.

1 mile

1 km

Kettlebury Hill with the trig point is in the same ridge as the Devil's Jumps - caused by an outcrop of ironstone. The other ridges of Hankley and Frensham Commons are gravel caps on the soft Greensand. These gravels are ancient tracts of the Blackwater River or its tributaries, the highest now 100m/300 feet above the present puny river. North of the Hog's Back at Caesar's Camp and Finchampstead Ridges the gravels form caps on the soft Bagshot Sands.

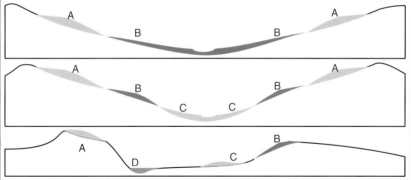

Torrents of melt water in the Ice Age a million years ago spread sheets of flint and sandstone shingle from the mountains of the Weald. Post-glacial rivers cut valleys with new shingle beds, leaving the old shingle as terraces above. The land rose and further valleys within valleys were cut in successive periglacial periods. Much of the older terrace material was carried off by rivers snaking through the soft sands to leave apparently random humps of gravel. Detective work by precise surveying has allowed the gravel to be related to their original terraces. The (Hythe) sandstone of the gravel S of the Hogsback suggests the water came from Hindhead; N of the Hogsback it is mainly flint out of the chalk. There appear to be eleven levels of terraces and old river beds can be deduced where no water flows now. The present and "fossil" rivers south of Farnham lead towards the present Blackwater Valley but the Wey captured them.

32 Thursley, Ridgeway Farm and Kettlebury Hill

About 9 km/5½ miles with an extension of 3¼ km/2 miles and a short cut of 3½ km /2 miles; shady and hilly, farmland and confusing heath, with wild but tranquil spots. OS maps 1:25000 133 Haslemere, 1:50000 186 Aldershot.

Start from Thursley recreation ground, SU 899 398 (park on the grass near the children's play area) or from a parking spot below Kettlebury Hill, SU 882 392.

Linking walks   29✳   30☆   31✳   33✿   ⟨15⟩✿   ⟨16⟩★   ⟨18⟩✿   ⟨19⟩✤   ⟨20⟩★

Three Horseshoes ☎ 01252 703268

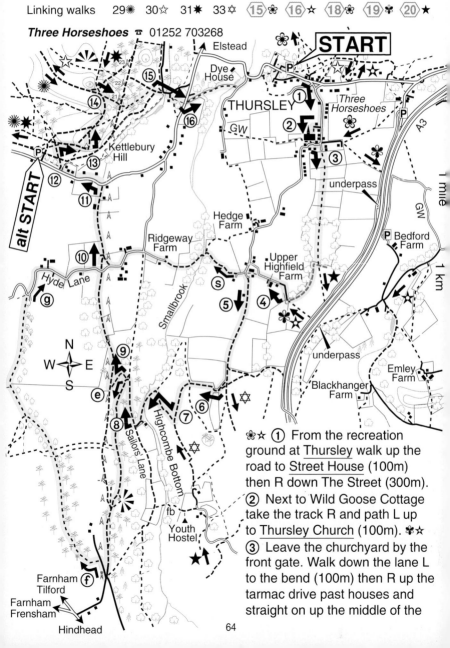

❀★ ① From the recreation ground at Thursley walk up the road to Street House (100m) then R down The Street (300m).

② Next to Wild Goose Cottage take the track R and path L up to Thursley Church (100m). ❀★

③ Leave the churchyard by the front gate. Walk down the lane L to the bend (100m) then R up the tarmac drive past houses and straight on up the middle of the

64

fields, stile to stile (450m). At the field ringed by trees, stay about 50m from the R edge (250m). ★ In the next field follow the track round the R edge into the dip (300m).

④ Join the farm track outside the field and go up R past a house and barns (350m). At the next bend diverge L on footpath through the stable yard, out to the road (100m).

Ⓢ *Short cut of 3½ km/2 miles: On the other side drop down the tarmac lane and track into the valley (300m). Cross Smallbrook, climb the rocky track to Ridgeway Farm (300m) and continue on the tarmac lane (150m). Stay ahead at the junction (Hyde Lane) up over the rise past Upper Ridgeway Farm and down into the next little valley (300m). Turn R down the track.* ➜⑩

⑤ Turn L. When the tarmac ends continue up the sandy track, disregarding side tracks L (800m). ✿

⑥ Bear R at the first fork, round the top of the field. Disregard the cross path after the field (350m) and stay on the main track curving L into the valley, down to the steeper side track back R (300m).

⑦ Turn back down the side track (300m) then bend L to Smallbrook (100m). Cross and carry on up the other side, past Keeper's Cottage to Sailors' Lane -the track from the Devil's Punchbowl fields (250m).

⑧ Turn R up the flank of the valley to the hairpin bend on top (350m).

ⓔ *Extension of 3¼ km/2 miles: Go L round the hairpin bend and along the main ridge track (1400m).*

ⓕ *At the telecommunications tower turn back R into the house drive (150m) then take the valley path L down to the lane (2100m).*

ⓖ *Go R on the lane over two ridges into the second valley (550m). Turn L down the track.* ➜⑩

⑨ Don't follow the hairpin bend or stay ahead but cross L over the ridge track into the next little valley with electricity pylons (200m) then follow the sandy track down R (800m) and cross Hyde Lane.

⑩ Keep on down (600m).

⑪ On the road go L (300m).

⑫ Turn R on the track after the cluster of 3 houses, bending ½L up to the ironstone ridge (200m). ✳✳ Turn R up the ridge track to the trig point on Kettlebury Hill (200m).

⑬ Turn L next to the trig point, down to the main track (100m). Stay ahead to the junction of major tracks on the next ridge (300m). Climb the small knoll for the view ☆ then return to the junction (200m).

⑭ Don't go off the sides but back along the ridge into the trees (200m). Pass the power lines R of pylon No 21 and keep on. Swing L onto the converging path over the brow of the hill (50m) and down to another track (150m).

⑮ Descend R (100m). At the junction carry on over the little stream and round R almost to the house, Hounmere (70m). Start up the path L of the garden but bear L immediately to scramble straight up the slope to the road (100m).

⑯ Carry on opposite along the footpath at the L edge of the field over the Dye House stream and down into the valley (400m). Walk down the lane L (100m) then R on the road (100m). When the road curves L keep on ahead up the path to the road, opposite the recreation ground (200m).

33 The Devil's Punch Bowl to Ridgeway Farm

About 9 km/ 5½ miles with a short cut of 3 km/2 miles; heath and woodland with hilly, stony paths; splendid views; best when the heather is in flower in August. OS maps 1:25000 133 Haslemere, 1:50000 186 Aldershot. The main road around the Punch Bowl will be removed after the A3 tunnel opens in 2011.

Start from the National Trust (pay) car park in Hindhead, SU 890 357.

Linking walks
32✡ ⟨19⟩ ❀ ⟨20⟩ ◆

Devil's Punch Bowl Hotel
☎ 01428 606565
Devil's Punch Bowl Café
☎ 01428 608771

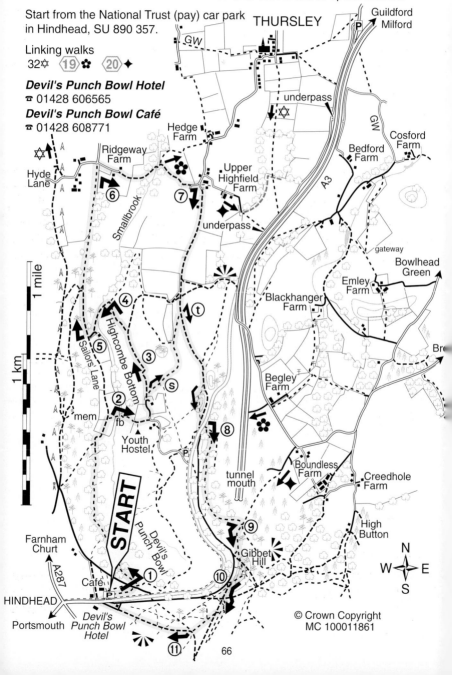

© Crown Copyright
MC 100011861

66

① From the NT car park walk over the grass, away from Hindhead, to the path on the rim of the Devil's Punch Bowl (150m). Continue on the rim (20m) then take the path down L into the wooded hollow. Eventually the path becomes a farm track past fields (1100m).

② After the first field R (150m) turn down the track R to the brook (100m). Cross and carry on up past the Youth Hostel to the tarmac drive (250m). Turn L down past Gnome Cottage (150m).

Ⓢ *Short cut of 3 km/2 miles: After the cattle grid take the path up R and follow the steep curve up the valley side, eventually past the corner of the small field (450m) to the ridge track on top (150m).*

Ⓣ *Turn L along the ridge. Join* ⑦.

③ Carry on along the track near the valley bottom, round a double bend (200m) and on up (300m).

④ On the broad R curve take the branch track down L (200m). Go L round the bend to Smallbrook (100m) and up past Highcombe Farm (150m) to the track from the fields - Sailors' Lane (70m).

⑤ Go R up the valleyside (350m). When the main track bends L on top, stay ahead on the path along the ridge, gradually sinking into a deep cleft between fields (900m). ✿

⑥ At Hyde Lane turn R up past Ridgeway Farm. Stay ahead on the rocky track down into the gorge (450m), over Smallbrook ✿ and up the other side. Continue on tarmac to the lane junction (300m). ✦

⑦ Turn R. Carry on up the track past the fields. Disregard tracks L, R & crossing (750m) and keep on up the stony track and along the ridge (600m). When level with the hillock in the trees L, diverge on the path over the hillock R (100m). ◥

> View: Eastwards are the Greensand hills, forming promontories out into the Weald. The isolated eminence is Hascombe Hill. Beyond it is the Leith Hill range. Left of it and closer is the cone of Hydon's Ball.
> To the north are two telecom towers almost aligned. The nearer one is 9km/5½ miles away, at Crooksbury Hill in front of the Hogs Back and the other is 26 km/16 miles away on Bagshot Heath above Camberley.

Descend ahead, back to the main track and the road (150m). (Major road until 2011 then narrow)

⑧ Cross slightly L into the wood to the path junction (30m) and take the side path R, up at first (100m), then gently undulating and winding round the hillside. Disregard an uphill fork R (350m) and keep on to the steep cross path (350m).

⑨ Turn R up Gibbet Hill, curving L. When the path flattens, ignore the side path R, cross a track (250m) then climb to the memorial cross and trig point (100m). ◥

⑩ At the trig point take the track away from the brow of the hill as if to join the hard track on the other brow of the hill (Old Portsmouth Road)(100m). Just before this bear L on the other track (100m). At the cross track take the little path ½ L and along the brow of the hill then turn R to the main track (100m) and cross obliquely. Keep on down to the T-junction on a bend (200m).

⑪ Go R round the L bend then stay ahead (South Downs visible L) all the way down to the car park in Hindhead (700m). The **Devil's Punch Bowl Hotel** is L (50m).

34 Waggoners Wells and Ludshott Common

About 7 km/4½ miles; an extension of 1½ km/1 mile and a short cut of
1½ km/1 mile can be used together; the numerous paths allow variation but
may cause confusion; heath, pasture and beechwoods; good in winter.
OS maps 1:25000 133 Haslemere, 1:50000 186 Aldershot.

Start from the Ludshott Common car park near Grayshott Hall, SU 852 358, or
from Waggoners Wells car park, SU 862 344.

The Fox & Pelican
☎ 01428 604757

HEADLEY DOWN

START

B3002

Churt

N
W—E
S

④
③

①
② Grayshott Hall

⑤
P

q

ⓢ

⑥

⑩

Ludshott Common

ⓟ

ⓞ

P

ⓣ

⑦

valley

North Lodge

valley

Waggoners Wells

alt START

Chase Farm

ⓔ
P

① At <u>Ludshott</u> Common
car park walk out to the
heath (40m). Go L on the wide
track down to the dip (300m).

ⓢ *Short cut of 1½ km/1 mile:*
Stay on the wide track over the
rise into the next dip (300m). Turn
down the valley (60m) and diverge
on the side path L, over to a very
oblique cross track (300m).

⑨

⑧ valley

ⓗ ridge track
brow path
valley track

ⓕ Bramshott

ⓖ Chase

P
Bramshott Common

P
A3 Bramshott

A3

ⓣ *Cross the junction into the trees*
(50m) and take the first side track L
to the hard vehicle track (200m).
There are two side paths opposite.
Take the L one, over another
vehicle track (20m) then ahead to
the edge of the valley and down to
the lane (600m). Cross the stream
to the bend (50m). ➔⑦

② After the little pond turn back L
into the trees. Keep on to the
road; turn R at the end (350m).

③ Follow the verge to the drive of
<u>Grayshott Hall</u> (100m) then go L on
<u>Hammer Lane</u> (200m). Opposite
the first house, turn R on the track.
Carry on until it bends R on the lip
of the valley (250m).

68

④ Just after it starts descending enter the field R and follow the L edge. Disregarding side paths, keep on to the track after a group of houses R (800m).

⑤ Turn R on the track to the sports field (30m). Cross diagonally to exit L of the pavilion (200m) and turn R to the main road (100m). Cross slightly L (30m) and go down the very steep drive. Drop off the end to the track junction in the valley bottom (200m).

⑥ Turn R down the valley (200m). Opposite the pump house bear L up the side path (80m) then branch R along the valley side (600m). At the end drop R to the tarmac lane (100m).

RAYSHOTT
Fox &
Pelican
P
Hindhead A3

⑦ At the bend in the lane take the path passing below Waggoners Wells car park. Drop to the dam at the end of the pond (150m) but stay ahead beside the second pond to the little side creek (200m).

Hindhead

ⓔ *Extension to Bramshott Common: At the side creek take the path L away from the ponds up the valley (400m) and fork R on the ascending track (150m).*

ⓕ *Over the top, join the ridge track and go L to the corner of the fields and Bramshott Chase (80m).*

ⓖ *Turn R on the path along the fence, inside or out, to the next cross path (200m). Turn R along this path which follows the brow of the hill parallel with the valley track visible below L (600m). Eventually the brow path swings R to join the ridge track (100m).*

ⓗ *Descend the ridge track L to its end where it meets the valley track converging from below L (600m).*

Make a U-turn R on the path round the end of the ridge (30m) and drop down the side path L to the footbridge (80m). ➤⑨

⑧ Continue along the pond to the end (60m) and ahead past the end of the next pond (250m) to a fork (100m) then descend R (100m).

⑨ Cross the footbridge and turn L up the flank of the valley. The horse track bends R and R again (200m). At the 2nd R bend take the footpath L up through conifers to the field (100m). Go on over the field (300m) and out through trees to Ludshott Common (100m). Cross the boundary track and go on (350m). On the track converging R continue ahead to the foot of the little rise (150m).

ⓞ *Slightly longer option (500m further): Go L on the side path down the valley (400m).*

ⓟ *At the corner of the field L bear R up over the ridge (250m). Just after the cross path, on the lip of the next valley fork R then L to the bottom (150m). Cross the valley track and go straight up the short steep slope (30m).*

ⓠ *Bear R up the cross track. Stay on this track round the edge of the open heath. It bends ½R (700m) then passes round the highest part and down to the car park (800m).*

⑩ Stay ahead over the little rise, past the next cross path (250m), to the L curve (50m) and turn R down the side track into the valley (200m). At the T-junction take a few steps R (10m) then continue in the previous direction, up a little side valley (800m). Near the top of the common turn R and continue to the car park L (300m).

35 The Basingstoke Canal and Tunnel Hill

About 9½ km/6 miles; canal and confusing pine wood tracks with short steep climbs; short cuts shown on the map; an extension of 1½ km/1 mile when red flags are not flying. OS maps 1:25000 145 Guildford, 1:50000 186 Aldershot.

Start from the verge of Mytchett Place Road outside the Basingstoke Canal Centre, SU 893 549, or the parking area near the minor road fork, SU 918 556. Ash Vale station has free parking at weekends, SU 893 534.

Linking walks 36✿ 37❀ 15❋ 16◈ 17★

Basingstoke Canal Centre ☎ 01252 370073
Range Office ☎ 01252 325233 8am-4pm
Potters ☎ 01252 513934

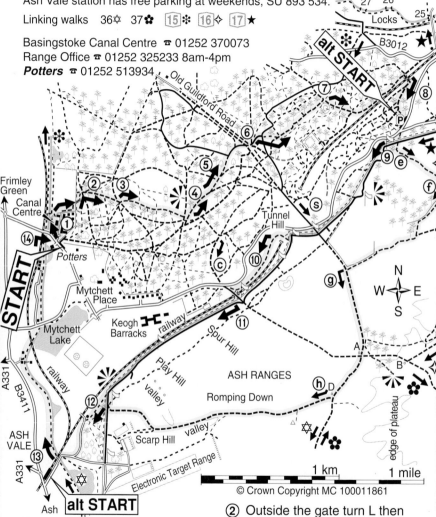

© Crown Copyright MC 100011861

① From the road walk through the canal centre diagonally L to the Basingstoke Canal). Follow it to the end of the side channel (250m). Turn R up the edge of the field to the R corner near houses (150m).

② Outside the gate turn L then diverge R from the fence to the multiple track junction (80m) and take the wide rising track directly away from the field (300m).

③ On the brow of the hill don't join the tracks R or ahead but bear L on

70

the descending track, which curves R then undulates up to a cross track on another brow (500m).

ⓒ *Short cut shown only on map.*

④ Go straight on through trees to the next track (40m) then L until a long track diverges L (250m).

⑤ Follow this side track. Disregard the tracks forking R and go on to join the hard track on a bend (250m). Stay ahead round R to a major junction (150m).

ⓢ *Short cut shown only on map.*

⑥ Cross the straight track (Old Guildford Road over Tunnel Hill) and take the hard track ahead round a R curve to another hard track at a bend (150m). Go over this track and down the steep foot-path (150m) then L on the next vehicle track to the end (450m).

⑦ Turn R and follow the track down, round a L curve (250m) then near the railway (600m). ★

⑧ At the bridge pass under the railway (50m) and turn back on the other side (40m). Don't keep on beside the railway but bear L up the sloping track. Disregard side paths until the junction of many tracks and paths (300m). Take the first path L up to the parking area near the road junction (100m). From the parking area walk up to the top corner of the road junction (100m) and cross both roads. Go up the heath track (20m). ✿✿✿

ⓔ *Extension of 1½ km/1 mile into* Ash Ranges *if red flags are not flying: Go down the curving track away from the boundary, through the valley (400m) and up round the R bends (200m).*

ⓕ *Carry on up to the end at the T-junction on the plateau (1000m).*

ⓖ *Turn L along the straight track. At a R curve disregard the lesser path forking L (550m) and keep on over the crossing track (70m)* ✿ *to the next major junction (350m).* ✿

ⓗ *Fork R and keep on over the plateau. Disregard the steep track back L after the bend (1700m) and go on to the 2nd steep track L next to the railway cutting (80m).* ➔⑫

⑨ Turn R along the boundary of the army ranges. If the red flags are flying stay on the footpath outside the fence. If not, use the track inside. Follow the undulating boundary over Longdown Hill (see London if clear) and Tunnel Hill where a major track crosses the boundary from the road (900m).

⑩ Carry on outside the boundary fence (200m). Just after the L bend take the path R over the tunnel mouth (100m) and follow the railway on the other side (500m).

⑪ Find the little path up to cross back at the next bridge. Continue along the boundary past Keogh Barracks R and up to the crest of Furze Hill (1100m). ✿ Don't fork L.

⑫ Outside the fence, drop down the path beside the railway cutting (250m). Stay ahead on the road, curving R. Cross the canal bridge beside the railway junction at Ash Vale Station and wharf (400m).

⑬ Follow the tow path under the railway. Keep on past Mytchett Lake (1000m), under a road bridge and ahead to the next road bridge (600m). ✳

⑭ Either ascend to the road and cross the bridge to the Canal Centre (100m) or stay on the tow-path (100m) and cross the Canal Centre footbridge.

36 Ash Ranges and the Basingstoke Canal

This walk is often not possible. Most days red flags are flown at entrances to the ranges 7am-5pm. Flags stay down some weekends and during Christmas, Easter and August holidays - Range Office 01252 325233.

About 8 km/5 miles with an extension of 1 km/¾ mile; over heath ridges; best in August and winter.   OS maps 1:25000 145 Guildford, 1:50000 186 Aldershot.

Start from the Ash Wharf car park opposite Victoria Hall (with clock turret), SU 896 515. At weekends, parking is free at Ash Vale station, SU 893 534.

Linking walks   35✿   37✤   38☆   16 ✳   43 ✳

The Swan ☎ 01252 325212   *The Standard of England* ☎ 01252 325539

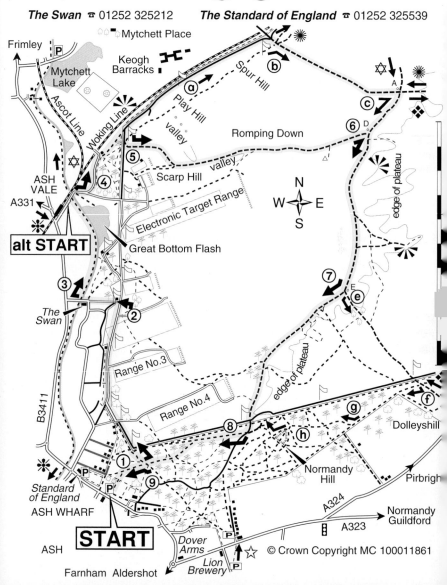

© Crown Copyright MC 100011861

✳① Take the path from the inner end of the car park, over a cross path after the tennis courts to an oblique T-junction (80m). Bear R up to a wide cross path (150m). The corner of the fence of Ash Ranges should be visible below L (100m). Walk down to it and enter. Stay ahead along the boundary track then on the road, past the ranges R and a house L (700m), to the top of the next rise (300m).

② Go out at the guard hut, down the drive, past the **Swan** and over the Basingstoke Canal (250m).

③ To follow the canal R (N) drop to the towpath. Pass Great Bottom Flash to Ash Vale Wharf just before road and rail bridges (750m). ✿

④ Cross the canal on the road bridge beside the rail junction at Ash Vale station. Follow the road down (150m) and take the L fork (300m). When the tarmac bends L at the pillbox continue up the gravel path. Keep on to the top (250m) and through the gateway. ↘

> **View**: The large buildings ahead are Keogh Barracks. The 12-storey block behind is the military catering school. Below L is Mytchett Lake. Mytchett Place is the white house in the trees visible between lake and barracks. On the skyline above the lake is the dome of Farnborough Abbey. The large house R of that is Farnborough Hill.

ⓐ *Alternative, slightly longer: Carry on ahead either on the boundary track or on the parallel path over the hills (1100m).* ✳

ⓑ *At the next major cross track, from the railway bridge, go R up to the next major cross track (950m).*

ⓒ *Go R to the major track fork (300m). Don't fork R.* ➜⑥

⑤ Turn back R on the track over the summit (80m). Avoid the next exit and curve L from the boundary on the track along the edge of Scarp Hill. Go on over the plateau to the end at the 3-way junction of major tracks (1700m). ❖ Turn R.

⑥ Stay on the same track to a major L fork (1100m). ☆ ↘

> **View**: Back L is Guildford Cathedral. It stands on a hill in front of the notch in the North Downs where the River Wey cuts through. The ridge R of the notch is the Hog's Back. The hill seen through the notch is St Martha's.

ⓔ *Extension of 1 km/¾ mile: Fork L down to the boundary (800m).*

ⓕ *Exit and turn R, not along the path beside the fence but the next one. Follow this over a rise (200m) and straight on down beside another fence L (350m).*

ⓖ *Turn R on a wide path (70m before a cart track L) and keep on round a L bend and up. Disregard all side tracks until the hill fort on top of Normandy Hill (500m).*

ⓗ *Go round or through the fort to the other end (100m) then turn R on the path to the boundary fence of the Ranges (200m). Follow the fence L to the gateway.* ➜⑧

⑦ Keep straight on but watch out for good views back L (1100m).

⑧ Go out from the boundary fence (60m) then turn R on the side path which soon descends. Disregard the side path L (170m) but fork L at the next large side path (200m). Carry on over a cross path (250m) and down to an oblique T-junction (fence corner visible R) (200m).

⑨ Slightly R (20m) take the small onward path (150m) and branch L to the car park (100m).

37 Normandy and the blasted heath

This walk is often not possible. Most days red flags are flown at entrances to the ranges 7am-5pm. Flags stay down some weekends and during Christmas, Easter and August holidays - Range Office 01252 325233.

About 8 km/5 miles mostly over open heath with steep and stony tracks; best when the heather is in flower (August) or during winter frosts and gales. OS maps 1:25000 145 Guildford, 1:50000 186 Aldershot.

Start from the car park at Normandy crossroads, SU 926 516.

Linking walks 35✿ 36❖ 37✽ 39✳ 40★ ④✳ 16◆

Duke of Normandy
☎ 01483 235157

Henley Park Range

1 km
1 mile

edge of plateau

Pirbri

A324

bog

works

Henley Park

fb

N
W　E
S

Dolleyshill

© Crown Copyright
MC 100011861

A324

Manor House

Duke of Normandy

Guildf

Ash
Aldershot
Farnham

A323

fb

P
P

NORMANDY

Wanborough
Hog's Back   Puttenham

START

✽① At Normandy crossroads take the path out of the corner of the car park over the footbridges and L of the tennis courts to the drive (250m). Cross the football field to the middle of the far edge (100m) and go on over or round the next field to the cricket pavilion (150m). Pass L of the pavilion to the path in the trees (50m). Follow the branch path outside the R edge of the next cricket field (or walk along the edge of the cricket field and join the path from the far end). Keep on round R up to the road (350m). Cross and follow the track up round the houses (120m).

② At the end of the wide track don't stay ahead but turn R up the track into the army land (300m). Cross the boundary track and fence and continue ahead to the top of the slope (750m). ❖

③ Just over the rim of the plateau, turn R on the major track. Ignore minor side tracks (unless in search of a picnic spot or view at the edge of the plateau). After the major side track back L (1100m), ❀ stay ahead to a cross track (300m). ✦

④ Turn R. Stay on this track and disregard all side tracks and paths. It soon descends from the plateau and undulates to the rifle range (1500m). Continue down the tarmac drive to the boundary gateway (500m). ☆

⑤ Just outside turn R on the track to Henley Park Lake (80m). Follow the footpath L around the edge of the lake (300m). Just over the bridge at the end, disregard the footpath R but go R on the horse track through the pine wood past a side track L (50m) and on to the oblique crossing track (170m). Bear L along this track almost to the road (250m). ❄❖

⑥ Don't join the road but bear R parallel with it to the boundary of the army land (30m) and ahead on the boundary track (600m).

⑦ Exit at the next gate L opposite Henley Park Farm (600m). Go on, R of the road, to the end of the L field (250m).

⑧ Cross just before the bend and follow the footpath at the edge of the field next to the wood, over the brow of the hill down to the corner (400m). Enter the small field ahead, cross the R corner and carry on down the R boundaries to the road at Hunts Hill Farmhouse (350m).

⑨ Turn R (40m). Opposite the next drive R, take the path L into the wood (40m). Just before the house, turn R over the drive (40m) and follow the branch path L down beside the garden. Keep on to Normandy crossroads (150m).

Heath occurs in low rainfall areas on sandy soils that lack calcium. Calcium is an essential nutrient for all plants but its absence also makes the soil hostile. Without it, humus does not gel on the sand particles - the gel would hold the water, nutrients and useful microbes. The pH is 4-5 because the humic acids are not neutralised by calcium. Only a few plants tolerate low calcium, acidity and dryness: bracken heathers and gorse. Hilltops are the most blown, drained and leached.

Heaths are "badlands" dating from the forest clearance by neolithic farmers. Intensive grazing by sheep and goats up to the early 20th century prevented forest regeneration. Previously, leaf fall in the oak forest provided copious humus and animals brought calcium.

The low rainfall and heathland belt stretches in an arc from East Anglia to Dorset. Around Farnham, heathlands abound. Northwards on the borders of Surrey, Hampshire and Berkshire the Tertiary (Bagshot) Sands and gravel terraces of the Ice Age rivers are the culprits. Southwards from the North Downs some of the Greensand strata are to blame: the Folkstone Sands in the band through Crooksbury Hill and the Hythe Sands through Gibbet Hill.

38 Normandy to Ash Green

About 8 km/5 miles over heath and fields with several stiles; a ½ mile extension if red flags are not flying. The heath section is rough with steep hills and boggy areas. OS maps 1:25000 145 Guildford, 1:50000 186 Aldershot.

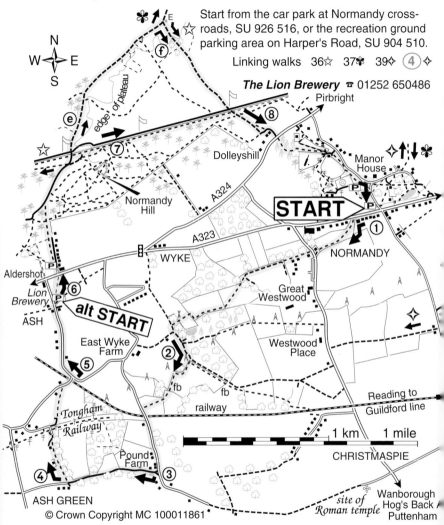

Start from the car park at Normandy crossroads, SU 926 516, or the recreation ground parking area on Harper's Road, SU 904 510.

Linking walks 36☆ 37❄ 39◇ ④ ◇

The Lion Brewery ☎ 01252 650486

© Crown Copyright MC 100011861

① From the <u>Normandy</u> car park cross the main road and turn R along the pavement (150m). After the car showroom, turn L into the field and cross to the far end. Pass L of the house to the road (400m). Slightly R (50m) take the footpath on the other side beside garden fences (200m). Stay ahead at the field (300m) then bear L through the trees to the next field (50m). Cross diagonally to the corner at the wood (200m) and go on beside it (250m). At the next field turn R with the path (40m) then L across to the trees and the track (150m).

76

② Turn L to the track junction (30m) and L along the larger track (220m). After the cables (30m) take the path R up the edge of the field, round into the corner then L to the next corner (250m). Over the ditch in the 2nd field, cut the corner R (35m) to the 3rd field and cross diagonally to the far gate (200m). On the road go L over the bridge (Tongham Railway) and on (450m).

③ At Pound Farm turn R along the track (600m).

④ At the tarmac road and 1st house L (in Ash Green) turn R on the path through the trees (300m). At the drive go R over the Tongham Railway cutting and its path (80m). After the bridge, go R down the drive then footpath to the next road (300m). Go R up over the Reading-Guildford railway bridge (100m).

⑤ Turn L down the road (500m). After the opposed houses enter the field R (or continue to the **Lion**).

⑥ From the parking area cross the field diagonally to the furthest corner (200m). Cross the main road and go up Nightingale Road (40m) then the path L of it (300m). Over the brow stay ahead to the hard track (150m). Turn R along this track to the army Danger Area of Ash Ranges (400m). ❀☆

ⓔ *Dry extension of ¾ km/½ mile if red flags are not flying: Cross the barrier and carry on up the ridge track. Ignore side paths (1100m).*

ⓕ *After the heads of 2 valleys R, take the next major track R down through the boundary (800m).* ➔⑧

⑦ Follow the boundary track R. When red flags are flying, follow the path outside the fence instead, down off the main hilltop and over several lesser ridges with boggy areas between them (1200m). At the next gate in the fence turn R.

⑧ Follow the track down (300m) and go L on the wide track round the house (120m). Cross the road and descend the footpath through the conifers (200m) then cross to the cricket field and go on along the L edge to the pavilion (200m). Walk around the L edge of the next cricket field and on along the belt of trees (250m). At the end go L to the road to see the Manor House, William Cobbett's last home (100m), then diverge back over the grass to the car park (250m).

William Cobbett, 1762-1835, was the most renowned journalist of his day. He was born into a farming family at the house which is now the *William Cobbett* pub in Farnham. His last home was the Manor House in Normandy. His grave is near the door of Farnham Church. In his youth he worked in the gardens of Waverley Abbey House, Farnham Castle and Kew. His father taught him to read and write and, inspired by Swift's *Tale of a Tub*, he went on to be a soldier, textbook author, journalist, farmer and MP. A child of Merrie England just before the industrial revolution he was to witness and rail against the relentless pauperisation of the farm workers which he blamed on paper money, decline of the landed gentry and demise of cottage industries. His journalistic outpourings, widely read by rich and poor, hastened reform but his excoriating pen drew bouts of prison and exile upon him. Gravitas eluded him because he was an egotist, maverick and reactionary but his prodigious, accurate and perceptive writings on everyday life and political machinations make him an important source for historians.   *William Cobbett* Richard Ingrams 2005 Harper Collins 333pp

39 Normandy, Henley Park and Merrist Wood

About 10 km/6½ miles mainly over fields; undulating; lots of stiles.
OS maps 1:25000 145 Guildford, 1:50000 186 Aldershot.

Linking 37✳ 38◇ 40✳ ①✚ ②✪ ③✿ ④✦ ⑥✳

Start from the car park at
Normandy crossroads,
SU 926 516.

Duke of Normandy
☎ 01483 235157

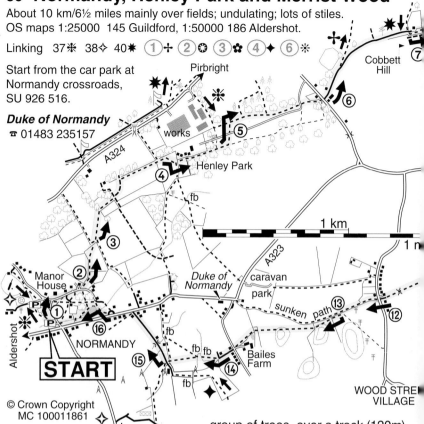

© Crown Copyright
MC 100011861

✳① Cross the footbridges from
the corner of the car park and walk
over the grass R of the tennis
courts converging on Hunts Hill
Road (150m). Cut the corner R to
follow the side road next to the
Manor House (300m).

② Turn L beside the drive of the
house at the R bend (Hunts Hill
Farm) and follow the path up the L
edge of the fields (350m).

③ Passing out of the small fields
don't continue up but turn R to the
corner (20m) then cross the fields
diagonally L towards the nearest
trees (200m). Pass below the next

group of trees, over a track (120m)
and up diagonally L to the gap in
the hedge (100m). Bear R on the
path R of the hedge towards the
houses at Henley Park (300m). ✳

④ Go round the bend and down a
little way (70m) then take the path
ahead below the gardens and up
through the wood (300m).

⑤ After the wood (100m) turn L on
the side path over the drive (150m)
and R along the parallel path at the
edge of the wood. This crosses the
drive (500m) and runs beside a
garden to the road (200m). ✛

⑥ Cross and carry on along the
track opposite across Cobbett Hill
to the house at the end (850m).

78

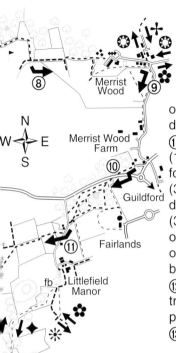

⑩ On the road double back R into the cul de sac (70m) and go on to the main road (150m). Cross to the verge opposite and go on round the end of the last garden into the wood (50m). Follow paths through the wood diverging from the road, over bridges and R of a pond to the tarmac drive at the furthest corner (450m). ❉✦

⑪ Walk along the drive L between fields (100m). Before the 1st house L cross the footbridge R and go straight over 3 fields (300m). In the 4th (with a track R), cross diagonally L to the middle of the top edge (300m). Pass over the top field in the same oblique line (200m) and out at the middle of the far edge. Follow the path down and between houses to the road (400m).

⑫ Cross the road and continue along the track opposite watching out for electricity poles L (150m) then a gate up L (100m).

⑬ Enter the field L and follow the hedge R over the hilltop then diverge slightly to the stile 30m L of the corner (200m). In the next field the right of way diverges from the R edge over the hillock and down to the pond R of Bailes Farm (400m). Follow the fence inside the field converging on the drive (170m).

⑭ Over the road, go on along the track between the houses (150m). When it bends R, cross the field ahead diverging from the L edge. After 2 footbridges (200m) ignore the R fork and keep on to the cart track near the barns (150m). ✧

⑮ Go R to the road (450m).

⑯ Walk along the pavement L (150m) then cross into the 2nd mouth of the track opposite. Take the path L (100m). After the bridge follow the edge of the pond to the far end. Keep on along the path which bends L to the road (200m) near Normandy crossroads (100m).

⑦ Turn R to the golf course fence and follow the onward path near it, eventually bending R (500m) to the cart track (150m).

⑧ Go L along the track (250m). When it bends R, carry on ahead on the path at the edge of the wood up to the Merrist Wood garden after the field (150m). The right of way is ahead up the edge of the trees (100m) and along the drive to the junction at the main buildings (300m) but the better route is R along the track outside the garden (100m), up L through the garden past the R end of the house and tennis court (200m) then ½R down across the corner of the field (200m). ♣✿

⑨ Turn R down the path beside the main drive, past the farm and the golf club gates and out past the lodges to the road (700m).

40 Pirbright to Henley Park

About 9½ km/6 miles or 1½ km/1 mile shorter if starting near Pirbright Lodge and missing the village; mainly level; woods and heath; boggy in wet seasons; shady in summer. OS maps 1:25000 145 Guildford, 1:50000 186 Aldershot.

Start from Pirbright car park on the green, SU 946 561, or near Pirbright Lodge, SU 938 551 (parking area at the end of the tarmac) or opposite the *Royal Oak*, SU 944 543 (layby at the end of the path).

Linking walks   37★   39✳   ①✳   ④★   17❀   3✳

The White Hart ☎ 01483 799715
The Cricketers ☎ 01483 473198
The Royal Oak ☎ 01483 232466

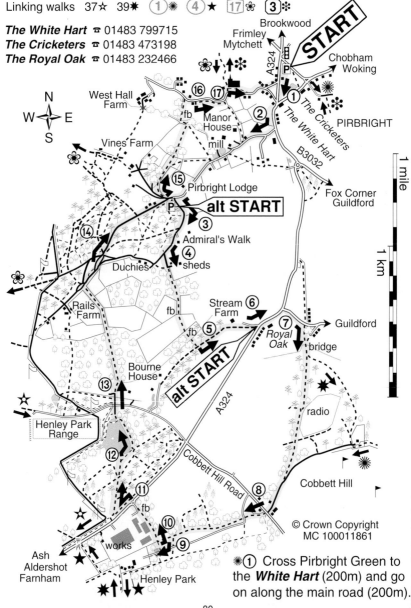

✳① Cross Pirbright Green to the **White Hart** (200m) and go on along the main road (200m).

② Turn R along Mill Lane. Keep onto the end of the tarmac passing the mill R and a large house R (Pirbright Lodge) (500m).

③ Go L up the cart track, Admiral's Walk, and down the other side of the hill (400m).

④ Take the first side track L (100m before the fork). After the sheds continue ahead on the path under trees and between fields to the end at a T-junction (550m).

⑤ Turn L and follow the path to the road (500m).

⑥ Cross the road and follow the pavement past the **Royal Oak** to the junction (250m) then R along Ash Road (200m).

⑦ Opposite the first houses L, take the path R (200m). Disregard the L fork after the cart bridge ✳ and keep on ahead (850m). At the top end converge on the boundary track outside the fields on Cobbett Hill and go on to the road (250m).

⑧ Cross the road and continue ahead on the footpath over a drive (200m) and beside trees (500m).

⑨ Take the path L (100m) then the tarmac drive R to the entrance of Henley Park house (200m). ★

⑩ After seeing the house retrace your steps (100m). Just after the mound L take the path L through the trees. Stay ahead past the buildings L (formerly Vokes factory) to the main road (350m). ☆

⑪ Cross the road to the parallel horse track in the wood and go L until almost opposite the centre of the main building (100m). Turn back R on the oblique horse track through the wood (not the vehicle track beside the fence). Disregard the side tracks (400m).

⑫ Just before the end bear R on the narrow path skirting Henley Park Lake. At the end join another path and continue beside the lake to the anglers' car park (300m).

⑬ Go straight out over the tarmac lane (80m) to the bend in the track under the trees (80m). Don't go round the bend but stay ahead on the path through the trees then between fields (800m).

⑭ At the cart track go R (150m). Where the track twists round the protruding corner of the field, fork L up the lesser track to the 6-way junction (80m) then keep to the main track ahead passing some houses with P (600m). ✿

⑮ Just before the tarmac turn back L on the track to Vines Farm but almost immediately (40m) bear R up the footpath under the trees (300m). On the hill carry on along the ridge top. Disregard a footpath down R and descend from the end of the hill slightly L to a corner (400m). Find the exit and follow the path L, over the footbridge and between fields to the road (200m).

⑯ Walk along the road R (60m). After the house R enter the field R but keep on near the road (200m).

⑰ Re-join the road at the bend and reach Pirbright Church via the path next to the house (100m). ❁ Continue along the churchyard to the furthest corner past the grave of Stanley, a large granite lump, then walk on along the road to the village green (400m).

x2

Devil's Coach Horse a beetle

Alice Holt Forest belongs to the Forest Commission; the land was bought in 1924. Most of it is open to the public for walking and riding. It is mainly oak and conifer plantations for commercial logging and research. *Holt* was Saxon for wood. *Alice* is thought to derive from the Saxon personal name, *Ælfsige*, diminutive *Alfsi*, possibly the Bishop of Winchester from 951. The Saxon hunting area which included Woolmer Forest, largely owned by the Bishops of Winchester, became one of the first designated forests under the Normans. The first keeper was probably Geoffrey the Marshal of the Domesday Book manor of Worldham since his de Venuz descendants were hereditary keepers. A record survives of the perambulation of the forest in 1171. The hammer beam roof of the Palace of Westminster was pre-fabricated at Farnham using Alice Holt oaks when it was re-roofed for Richard II in 1394. A survey of 1608 declared 13,031 trees suitable for the Royal Navy. Alice Holt ware is the archæologists' name for pottery from the huge Roman Pottery works.

Alice Holt, its history & potteries A G Wade & W Lowther British Archæology 1949 47pp

Alice Holt Lodge is now a research station of the Forestry Commission with laboratories, library and trial plots, complementing the work of the northern station near Edinburgh. The research and advisory service covers propagation, pathology and breeding of trees, pest control, ecology and recreation. The house dates from about 1816 and was a military hospital in WWII before the Forestry Commission bought it in 1946. The medieval Great Lodge for the Ranger or Lieutenant of the Forest may have been here though Gilbert White thought it was at Jenkyn Place in Bentley. Sir William Sandys wrote of living in the Great Lodge in 1530 when he was Henry VIII's Ranger. Ruperta Howe, daughter of Prince Rupert and actress Peg Hughes, was Ranger from 1709. Her husband introduced boar and buffalo which the locals promptly killed.

The **Army waterworks** appear to have been started around 1865, ten years after the army came to Aldershot. They were used until recently because they supplied water more cheaply than the public utility. Runnels around Cæsar's Camp and Beacon Hill catch run off and take it to ponds. The small plant near the bottom reservoir treated it and pumped it to the circular covered reservoir.

Ash Ranges is used by the army for rifle shooting. The target areas are all set against hillsides but people are kept out on firing days as a precaution against stray bullets. The house obtruding on the west boundary was built as a private enterprise tea shop for soldiers. The land is on the Tertiary (Bagshot) Sands. The most extensive plateau is the 8th Ice Age gravel terrace of the proto-Blackwater River from about 600 000 years ago (Anglian Glaciation).

Barrows are burial mounds. In this area all are bowl barrows of the Bronze Age (approx 2500 - 700 BC). They usually had ring ditches - often detectable only by excavation - giving them the profile of an inverted bowl. All have been plundered. The early ones had burials; the later ones, urns with cremated remains. Surviving barrows are often in prominent positions, apparently on territorial boundaries. Many will have been lost to the plough and erosion.

Bat's Hogsty is a curiosity amongst walkers because of its name and because they cannot find it; amongst archæologists because they cannot decide what it was for. It is a rectangle of about ¾ acre enclosed by four mounds with three ditches between them, externally 300' x 270', in total about 1¾ acres.

The Bat's Hogsty Earthworks D Westlake Aldershot Hist & Arch Soc 1983 & 84

The Basingstoke Canal, 37 miles long, is owned jointly by Hants and Surrey County Councils. It started from the Wey Navigation at Byfleet in 1796 at the peak canal building period. Not linking areas of industry and dense population it was perceived as the first agricultural canal - food to London, horse dung and coal to the country. It did not pay for itself. The last large contract was to carry bricks from Up Nateley for the re-building of Aldershot army camp at the end of the 19th century. The last barge tied up at Basingstoke in 1910.

London's Lost Route to the Sea P A L Vine 1973 David & Charles 267pp

Batt's Corner is a hamlet of Dockenfield. A Henry Bat is listed in a rental of 1222. Perhaps it was his corner of land.

Beacon Hill has similar terrain to Cæsar's Camp. The trig point was erected in 1951. The beacon appears in Norden's map of 1595, part of a county network fanning out from the Isle of Wight. Beacons told of the fall of Troy in 1084BC. In England the earliest record of beacons is in 1324 when Edward II prepared for invasion. *The Beacon System in Hampshire* H T White Proc Hants Field Club Vol X 28pp

Bentley in Hampshire was in ancient times a berewick of the great Manor of Farnham in Surrey, given to the Bishops of Winchester with a charter of King Cædwalla in 688. BENEDLEI in the Domesday Book was the 10 hides held directly by the bishop and two small manors of Osbern and William. There was a mill taxed at 10s but no church is listed. Before the by-pass opened in 1994, the main road through the village was the A31 following the line of the Pilgrim's Way from Winchester to Canterbury, sharing its ancient traffic with the Harow Way along the ridge north of the village. The Open Book near the cross roads was designed by Baden Powell who lived at Pax Hill 1918-1938.

Bentley Church, St Mary the Virgin, dates from around 1170. Features of interest: Norman north pillar, chapel and tower of about 1180; south chapel of about 1240, 12th century font bowl in Purbeck marble, 19th century table tombs, remarkable yews, carpets of snowdrops in February. It did not have a rector until 1864. The tithes were allocated to Waverley Abbey which supplied preachers. After the Dissolution of the Monasteries the tithes went to the Archdeacon of Surrey who kept up the tradition with a perpetual curacy. Jane Austen's brother, Henry, was the curate in 1816, living at the Old Parsonage.

Bentley Mill, also known as Turk's Mill, was a three storey brick building demolished early in the 20th century. The present building was the millhouse.

The **Blackwater River**, now puny, rises on Rowhill, Aldershot, and joins the Loddon at Swallowfield, forming the Hampshire boundary with parts of Surrey and Berkshire. It was the ancient main river of the district from Hindhead to the sea via the valley eventually taken over by the Thames later in the Ice Age.

Bourne Mill dates from the 17th century. It had two overshot wheels powered by the unreliable Nadder Stream from Farnham Park. The last working miller, Aldred Simmons, retired in 1900. The building was cut back for road building in the 1920s. It is now an antiques shop.

Bramshott was the Domesday Book manor BRENBRESETE whose common land was part of Woolmer Forest, a Saxon royal hunting area. The many tracks on the flat part of Bramshott Common were for a large Canadian Arrmy camp in WW2. Grey sandstone protruding in steep tracks is part of the Hythe beds of the Lower Greensand and is seen in a few house walls eg Chase Farm.

Cæsar's Camp: The view: Below is Farnborough Airport tower. Above it on the skyline is the telecommunications tower on the Bagshot Heath ridge. At the L end of this ridge is Broadmoor. Standing with both towers in line, the Wembley arch and London buildings are very slightly R. Guildford Cathedral is further R in front of the North Downs notch occupied by the River Wey and the town. 100m below is the later Ice Age valley of the proto-Blackwater River. Underfoot flints spill out from a 4m pebble layer which was the bed of the river earlier in the Ice Age (pre-Anglian, perhaps 1m years old). The flints of nearby buildings were supplied from the quarry on the south side. Cæsar's Camp is an Iron Age promontory fort of about 28 acres. The flat parts have well preserved double and treble ramparts but the scarp is so steep it was probably not fortified. No major excavation has been made. A small trench showed a defence mound had six layers and post holes which may be the remains of the medieval pale of the Bishop's park. The Battle of Farnham, 893 in the Anglo-Saxon Chronicle, is said to have taken place on low ground below Cæsar's Camp. After Alfred the Great made peace with Viking settlers, a group of Viking raiders landed in Kent. He placed an army to stop them breaking out. When they did, he fought and beat them here, recaptured booty, then chased them over the Thames.

Charles Hill estate, owned by the Lewson-Gore family in the 19th century, was split up within the family. The grim ironstone of the cottages is relieved by quaint shapes, magnificent barge-boards and cream-coloured quoin and coping bricks. Firbank Cottage, built around 1820 was the coach house.

Compton first appears in a charter of 727 when sub-king Frithuwold of Surrey gave to Chertsey Abbey, 4 hides at Comptone. In the Domesday Book it is CONTONE, a manor of 14 hides. Early in the 13th century it was split into the Manors of Down (north of the Hog's Back), Polstead, Field Place, Westbury and Eastbury, still represented by large houses of these names. The *Harrow Inn* has been licensed since at least 1780. The double jettied 15th century house, White Hart, was a pub before 1780, and possibly the church ale house. The church, St Nicholas, has a Saxon tower of flint and bargate, so is probably on the site of the Domesday Book church. The nave walls were replaced by hard chalk pillars when aisles were added about 1160. The Norman doorway, font, lozenge mural over the chancel arch and coloured glass in the E window are 12th century work. The chapel over the sanctuary is very unusual and its wooden guard rail exceedingly ancient. A Crusader graffito is scratched on the south jamb of the chancel arch. The shingled spire is 14th century.

The History of Compton in Surrey Lady C Boston 1987 Compton P C 247pp

Crondall was the Saxon Hundred, CORENDEL, made up of the manors of Crondall (CRVNDELE), Cove, Itchel, Farnborough, Long Sutton and Badley. It appears in Alfred the Great's will, drafted *circa* 885, as a bequest to Ethelm, his nephew. *He* passed it to St Swithun's Abbey, Winchester. After the Dissolution in 1539, it was granted to the Dean & Chapter. The roads reflect the Saxon layout; there are houses of all periods from 1475. The *Plume of Feathers* on its prime site was probably always an inn. The jettied part dates from about 1500; the middle part would have replaced an earlier hall house a bit later. The front parlour has a dragon beam to support the joists for jettying on two sides and the corner. It is said Cromwell stayed in October 1645, on the way to the siege of Basing House.   *Medieval Houses in Crondall* M A Jeffries *Crondall Society News*

Crondall Church, All Saints, was built in the 12th century when styles were changing, with Norman round arches in the nave but slightly pointed arches in the chancel. The clerestory arches are Victorian brick restorations. Features of interest: the east end of the aisles distorted by the original central tower (replaced by the brick north tower in 1657 for £428), the slanting chancel arch pillars, the possible Saxon font, a fine brass of about 1380 in the chancel floor.

Crooksbury Common was enclosed in 1855 and parts sold for building. The undeveloped area is owned by the Forestry Commission. The tracks are open to the public and good for walking. It has several Bronze Age barrows.

Crooksbury Hill is a Lower Greensand hill. The name may be trilingual repetition, *crug*, Celtic for hill, and *beorg*, Saxon for hill. The trig-point was built in 1951 for the 3rd triangulation of Britain and was levelled in 1974 (162.55m). Flint chippings from the summit suggest there was a mesolithic camp nearby. The little hill fort on the north flank, Soldiers' Ring, may be Bronze or Iron Age. The Crooksbury Hoard of bronze tools was found nearby in 1857 and a bronze axe head in 1954. The telecommunication tower on the adjacent Stone Hill is the Air Traffic Control link between Swanwick and Heathrow.

Cutt Mill crossroads takes its name from the mill at the south end of the pond which was there in 1273 when it was part of the marriage settlement of John le Cotte's daughter to John le Paumer. The mill turned until the 1930s but all that remains are pillars and a shed; the present house was the mill cottage.

The **Devils's Jumps**, three hillocks, are outcrops of carstone (ironstone). Two of them are on private land.

The **Devil's Punch Bowl** is a large combe set in the side of Gibbet Hill. The name first appears in Rocque's *Map of the County of Surrey* of 1765 and was probably the product of Georgian romanticism. Earlier names were Highcombe and Haccombe. *Hegcumbe* in a charter of 909 may derive from hay growing in the fields where the bottom has been cut down to the Atherfield Clay. The clay raises the water table into the sides. The springs sap the Hythe beds which are largely unlithified sands but the sides remain steep because this is a low rainfall area and the sand causes absorption rather than run-off. Grey freestone seams stabilize the higher parts and may have been dug out of the slopes.

Dippenhall is a hamlet of Wrecclesham but has wandered in its attachments being a tithing of Farnham in the 14th century but of Crondall in the 15th.

Dockenfield was a Hampshire tithing of Frensham in Surrey. There was a Doccenaford in the Charter of 909 defining the boundaries of the Farnham Hundred. Waverley Abbey had a license from Edward II to assart there.

Elstead must have existed at the time of the Domesday Book but is not listed because its tax data was lumped with the rest of the great manor of Farnham. The first mention is in the 1128 founding charter of Waverley Abbey when two acres of HELESTED were donated by the Bishop of Winchester. The Old houses are the 16th century Peace Haven & Lilac Cottage in Milford Road; Domford in Thursley Road, Old Farmhouse in Farnham Road. The forge on the green dates from 1686. Peter Sellers and Ringo Starr lived at Brookside. Fullbrook is a Lutyens house. Elstead bridge is attributed to the Waverley monks in the 14th century but has been renovated several times. The new part was added in WWII. *Elstead Then & Now* Gillian Drew 2001 81pp

Elstead Church, St James, was a chapel of Farnham by 1291 but the fabric suggests it was started in the middle of the 12th century. Built of bargate and chalk, the 14th century parts still visible are the blocked doorway in the chancel, the pointed chancel arch and the middle window in the north wall.

Elstead Mill is now a restaurant. The building dates from about 1800. When operations ceased in 1881 it was making worsted fringes. In the 17th century it had been a corn, malt and fulling mill and the previous building was put up in 1648. Helstede mill's rent was 10s 3d in the Bishop's pipe roll of 1208 so it is probably on the site of one of the six Domesday Book mills of Farnham.

Ewshot was hived off as a parish from Crondall and Crookham in 1886. It first appears in records of 1279 as land of the Bishop of Worcester - a Giffard. The church, St Mary's, suits this period but is Victorian (built 1873).

Farnborough Abbey has a small community of monks. The abbey church in Flamboyant Gothic style was built for the Empress Eugenie in the 1880's as a mausoleum for Napoleon III and their son Prince Louis who was killed in the Zulu Wars. She lived at the grand house on the adjacent Farnborough Hill, originally built for Longman the publisher and now a girls' school.

Farnham is a site of ancient habitation. Numerous palæolithic flint tools have been collected in the gravel pits and there were mesolithic pit dwellings at a chalk spring east of the Park. It was an important centre of the Roman pottery industry. One of the earliest Saxon charters marked the grant in 688 by King Cædwalla of Wessex to the Abbey of Winchester of the Farnham estate which became the large Domesday Book manor and hundred. The estate accounts are intact from the 12th century because of the episcopal ownership and are an important historical source. Farnham became a major hop centre after 1597. Daniel Defoe described it as the greatest corn market in England in 1722. It was a coaching town halfway between London and Portsmouth; the Lion & Lamb Yard is a 1980s development on the site of the Lamb Inn. Castle Street is a fine example of Georgian townscape, almost every house being a listed building. William Cobbett was born in 1763 at the pub which now bears his name; his grave is next to the church porch. The Maltings were bought by public subscription in the 1960s as an arts centre but are on the site of an ancient brewery. The church, St Andrew's, is probably on the site of the 7th century minster endowed by King Cædwalla. The present malmstone building was founded in the 12th century but has been much altered and enlarged.

Mediæval Farnham Etienne Robo 1980 Langam 326pp

Farnham Castle (☎ 01252 721194) is the Centre for International Briefing which prepares people for work and life overseas. The main rooms are open to the public on Wednesday afternoons. The Castle Keep, (English Heritage ☎ 01252 713393) is open summer afternoons Fri-Su.The late 12th century wall encloses the early Norman motte (mound) with the foundations of the tower, 15m square, built by the third Norman Bishop of Winchester, Henry de Blois, who was a grandson of William the Conqueror and brother of King Stephen. The curtain wall, gate house and domestic buildings date from around 1300 but are much altered. During the Civil War William Waller captured the Castle in December 1642 and used it as his HQ. It became the main residence of the later bishops until 1927, then bishops of the new See of Guildford until 1955.

Farnham Old Park is no longer an entity but gives it name to various farms etc. A parker is mentioned in the Bishop's accounts for 1210 but it very likely had Saxon antecedents. The castle was probably sited in it. Crown documents of 1284 record Edward I resolving, at Caernavon, a hunting dispute between bishop and abbot. James I hunted here after his coronation at Winchester. The two parks were sold off for £8145 after the Civil War but retrieved at the Restoration. Bishop Morley disparked the Old Park around 1670.

Farnham Park was made for the Bishop of Winchester William of Wyckham in 1376. Bishop Morley (1662-84) built the Ranger's House for his nephews - now a private residence. The Church Commissioners offered the Park to Farnham Town in 1928 with a choice of £10,000 and a covenant against building or a very much higher price were it to be used for building. The Castle ridge is on the chalk. The upper parts are on the London Clay hence the bogginess.

Frensham is a group of hamlets and isolated houses, not a compact village. It does not appear in the Domesday Book because it was taxed as part of the great Farnham estate of the Bishops of Winchester. The parish formed the corner of Surrey between Sussex and Hampshire until Shottermill (1845) and Churt (1865) became separate parishes.

Frensham Church, St Mary the Virgin was built in 1239, for the Annals of Waverley Abbey record *The Chirch of Fermesham has been moved this year from the place where it was first sited.....* Points of interest: the lancet window, priest's door, aumbry and piscina in the chancel, all of the original church but covered by a 19th century timber roof, 14th century tower, 15th century porch, the north aisle added in 1827 with an arcade older in style than the church, the nave windows of the 1868 restoration. The cauldron is said to have come from Mother Ludlam's cave.

Frensham Common like most West Surrey commons is largely heath lying on the Lower Greensand. The 998 acres of public open space were amassed by the local authority and the National Trust from bequests and purchases from 1925 onwards and all transferred to NT ownership in 1970.

Frensham Great Pond is fed by a stream from Churt and drains to the Wey. It would have been dammed in Saxon or early medieval times for fish-farming. The earliest reference is a payment of 14½d to Walter the fisherman in 1208 in the bishop's pipe rolls. In 1210-11 he was paid 11s 4d for fishing and carting (live) fish to London and to Wolvesey Castle, the bishop's Winchester home. The last quinquennial emptying of the pond to harvest the fish took place in 1860.   *Frensham Then & Now* H Baker & H Minchin 1948 Langam 175pp

Frensham Little Pond (Tancred's Mere) lay in the great manor of Farnham which belonged to the Saxon Bishops of Winchester for four centuries before the Domesday Book. The pond is clearly dammed and would have been made for fish-farming. When it started is unknown but in 1248 the tenants were disputing with the bishop payment for building work on it.

Frensham Mill closed in 1920 and the Victorian building (1876) was pulled down two years later. All that remains is the mill house, granary and water tunnel. Rocque's map of 1768 shows it and the Bishop's rent rolls indicate it existed in 1217. Frensham Great Pond effectively acted as the mill pond.
The Watermills of Surrey Derek Stidder 1990 Barracuda Books 144pp

Frowsbury in the Puttenham Heath golf course is a Bronze Age mound. It may gets its name from a landowner, de Frollesbury. A plaque indicates Queen Victoria visited in July 1858; she was reviewing troops on exercise.

Gatwick is a fairly common name from the Saxon for goat farm. It suggests that heathland was the dominant vegetation.

Gibbet Hill is the second highest hill in Surrey. The trig point at 272m/895' was one of the primary series erected in 1936 for the triangulation of Britain which began that year. Most trig points are now redundant but this one is retained as a reference point for GPS. The track skirting the brow of the hill, now with hard surface was the old Portsmouth Road. The cutting below was for the old A3 later diverted through the tunnel to open in 2011. The sailor's stone marks the place where the body of the murdered sailor was found in 1786. Dickens has Nicholas Nickleby reading the inscription to Smike as they walk to Portsmouth. The Celtic Cross on top was set up in 1851 by Lord Chief Justice Earle on the site of the gibbet when it fell. After execution the sailor's murderers were hung on this gibbet in 1787. Their bodies would have been tarred for preservation.

POST OBITUM SALUS After grief, salvation,   IN OBITU PAX In death, peace
POST TENEBRAS LUX After darkness, light   IN LUCE SPES In light, hope

The **Greensand Way**, GS, was officially opened in 1980. It is a 110 mile path from Haslemere, Surrey to Hamstreet, Kent.

Grayshott Hall is a mansion which grew to its present form in 1887. The village developed in the 19th century from a hamlet on the edge of Headley Parish but now has its own church.

Hampton may have taken its name from dower land for Alice de Hampton of Oxfordshire who married Walter de Puille, Lord of the Manor of Tongham, in 1268. The house is Georgian, built about 1760, but was frenchified around 1890 by upwards extension into a mansard roof.

Hankley Common belongs to the army but is open to the public for walking and riding. It used to be used for parachute exercises but army activities are now infrequent. Because of its expanses of heather and its ridges it is one of the most pleasant Surrey heaths, continuous with the heath of Witley, Thursley and Frensham Commons.

The **Harow Way** was the medieval high road from Winchester to Farnham, continuing as the Pilgrim's Way in Surrey, probably a pre-historic trade route. It is said to be the Tin Road from Cornwall to Kent and the Continent.

Henley was Henlea in a charter of Frithwold, king of Surrey in 727, granting 2 mansae of land to Chertsey Abbey. Domesday Book HENLEI was *given to the Abbey by Azor for his soul's sake in the time of King William, as the monks say.* The estate was the land between Frimley and Ash and the River Wey. It was leased to the crown in medieval times - the rent included 12 gallons of honey. For 700 years courtiers lived at Henley, including Reginald Bray who found Richard III's crown (for Henry IV) at Bosworth. Queen Mary granted Henley to Lord Montague who lived here and provided a home to recusants and priests but was sufficiently esteemed by Elizabeth I to be employed as a diplomat. The last resident was Lord Pirbright . Mr Vokes purchased the estate in 1940 to replace his bombed Putney factory. The present manor house was built in 1751 and converted to apartments in 1998.   *The History of Henley Park* Vokes 21pp

High Mill existed in 1288 for in that year the tenant miller, William Blyas, was evicted and fined 20s. There is a reference to it in 1692 as a fulling mill. It ceased public milling around 1900 but continued in private use for animal feed and as a sawmill until 1950. The wheel was internal.

Hindhead developed along the London to Portsmouth road on the edges of Thursley, Frensham and Haslemere parishes and Hampshire. In the middle of the 19th century, it was three cottages and an inn, *The Royal Huts*. The Gibbet Hill tunnel (2011) takes the A3 away from the centre. The Devil's Punch Bowl Hotel was the country house of the Hon. Rollo Russell, son of Lord John.

The **Hog's Back** is the part of the North Downs where the contortion of the strata is greatest - the bedding in one of the chalk pits has a dip of 60°. The name first appears in a letter of 1802 quoted by Mowbray Howard in *The Longs of Jamaica and Hampton Lodge*. It was still *Guildown* in Gilbert White's diary in 1797. The road is from Winchester to Guildford and may be the oldest road in Britain. The Hog's Back Hotel is on the site of an ancient beacon and the Poyle Hill Admiralty semaphore station in the line to Plymouth, between Worplesdon and Binsted.

Horsedown Common despite its name is part of a farm. The hill is an outlier of the London Clay standing proud on the chalk.

Itchel, now a small cluster of houses and farm, was taxed for 8 hides in the Domesday Book as the holding TICELLE & COUE (Cove) within the Abbey of Winchester's Hundred of Crondall.

Keogh Barracks has a museum of the army medical services which is open to the public (01252 868612). This is the Defence Medical Services Training Centre (Army, RN and RAF). It started during the First World War as a hutted camp for training soldiers then became a military police HQ. The permanent buildings were put up in the 1930s for the Army School of Hygiene and were augmented in the 1960s and 80s for the RAMC (Royal Army Medical Corps). QARANC (Queen Alexander's Royal Army Nursing Corps) moved in in 1994. Sir Alfred Keogh (1857-1936), a Dubliner, was Director General of Army Medical Services before and during the First World War.

Kettlebury Hill is a carstone (ironstone) protuberance in the same line as the Devil's Jumps. The trig point was built in 1950 as a subsidiary survey point for the triangulation of Britain which had begun in 1936. The long spur ridge to the Lion's Mouth and Yagden Hill is soft sand capped by river terrace gravel of the proto-Blackwater, with fragments of Hythe Sandstone from the Hindhead area.

King's Ridge and the adjacent hilltops on Frensham Common are protected by a cap of gravel, terraces of the "fossil" tributary of the River Wey.

Long Sutton was SUDTUNE in the Domesday Book. With a charter of 979 King Ethelred restored Long Sutton to Bishop Ethelwold for the Crondall estate. A wolf pit is mentioned as a boundary mark in the same document. The village street is the Harow Way or Tin Road. The church, All Saints, is 13th century, built of flint and chalk rubble. Features of interest: the narrow lancet windows at the east end - not replaced as in most churches by a large Tudor east window, the font and the great wooden chest in the chapel - both probably as old as the church, the oak pillars supporting the 15th century bell turret. The west window, chancel arch and external buttresses are 19th century work.

Lord Wandsworth College lies in the midst of its own farmland. It was founded under the will of Sidney James Stern (1844-1912), banker and MP, who gave generously to the Liberal Party and became Lord Wandsworth. Old boys are *Sternians*. 700 acres were bought in 1914 and the first boys joined in 1922. The bequest was for an orphanage but the trustees set up an Agricultural College for orphans who worked on the land as well as books. It transformed itself into a public school and dropped *Agriculture* from the name in 1938.

Ludshott is now part of Bramshott Parish but was the Domesday Book manor LIDESETTE. It has only a scatter of isolated houses SW of the Common. The heath of the Common is due to the Hythe Sands of the Lower Greensand.

Lydling Farmhouse is a Grade II listed building, a Queen Anne house built soon after 1700. The name is ancient, occurring in a pipe roll of 1177; it might derive from *hlinc*, Saxon for bank of a brook called Lyd.

A **Lynchet** is a step on sloping ground on the line of an ancient hedge. The cause is soil creep down to the hedge, and away from it below, largely due to ploughing. Lynchets are indicative of field systems as early as the Bronze Age.

Merrist Wood house was designed by Norman Shaw in 1877 but has been extended and ravaged by fire. Surrey County Council acquired the estate by compulsory purchase for a mental institution but WWII intervened and it became a Farm Institute instead when counties were obliged to provide training in agriculture. 23 students joined in 1945 but more than 1000 now enrol and courses have diversified: horse management, golf studies, sports turf management, landscaping, garden design, arboriculture, conservation, etc.

The **Moat** pond is used for radio-controlled sailing dinghies, hence the buoys. It is absent from maps until the early OS editions so may have been dug in the mid 19th century, possibly as a duck pond. The origin of the name is obscure.

Monks' Hatch, now the name of a house, would have been one of the ways to the farm when the Cistercians of Waverley Abbey owned Wanborough; its farmland stretched over the Hog's Back. The heavy-looking bridge was by Lutyens for the Compton A3 bypass of 1931 ornamented with crosses where it flies over the Pilgrim's Way. The new bridge for the A3 opened in 1989.

Moor Park House was Compton Hall when built in 1650. It was adapted under its present name in 1684 as a retirement home for Sir William Temple, 1628-99, a diplomat of Charles II. He is credited with the Triple Alliance and the match of William & Mary but his secretary from 1688, Jonathan Swift, is now more famous. Swift's early satire, *The Tale of the Tub*, was written here. Sir Walter Scott was a 19th century visitor and the novel *Waverley* (1814) probably owes its name to his visits. Charles Darwin visited in the 1850s for a health cure when it was a hydropathic establishment and liked it for the local walks.

The **murdered sailor** was never identified. Walking to Portsmouth in 1786 he fell in with three others at Godalming. They had no money and he agreed to fund them for the journey. They were last seen together in the *Red Lion* at Thursley. They murdered him on Gibbet Hill at the spot marked by the stone. The thugs were arrested in Rake, trying to sell his belongings. Their bodies hung for years on Gibbet Hill. The sailor's grave is at Thursley church. Baring Gould's Hardy-esque novel *The Broom-squire* tells of the sailor's fictional baby daughter and relates to local places at Thursley and the Devil's Punch Bowl.

Mother Ludlam's Cave in the Greensand cliff of the Wey has not been linked to a person of that name. Perhaps a poor widow lived here in the 18th century. The cauldron in Frensham Church is reputed to have come from here.

Mytchett was le Mucheleshette in 1340 when listed as a farm in the inventory of Chertsey Abbey. The name probably derives from *large corner*; this is the corner of Frimley Parish.

Mytchett Place, previously Mitchett Lodge, was built as a family home in 1779. The War Department bought the estate in 1912 and used the house as a residence for generals. It became an Army Medical HQ in 1960 but was sold off in 1983 and is now owned by Frazer Nash, who build and test electric cars in the grounds. In 1941 it was fortified as Camp Z for 13 months, the secret prison of Rudolph Hess (1894-1987), Deputy Fuehrer under Hitler - later dubbed "Squire of Mytchett" by a local newspaper. The State papers are withheld for 100 years but it is said he piloted an aircraft to Scotland to try and arrange peace. He was held in the Tower of London before Mytchett then at Abergavenny Mental Hospital and finally Spandau, Berlin.

Normandy is not an ancient village. It may have taken its name from a *Duke of Normandy* inn. There are two splendid 16th century houses, Westward Place and Great Westwood. The Manor House is an 18th century building. It was Normandy Farm leased by William Cobbett and it is here that he died.

The **North Downs Way**, a modern concoction for walkers, designated by the Countryside Commission in 1978, runs 153 miles from Farnham to Dover.

Odiham has a delightful, wide High Street with buildings of many periods. The settlement is very ancient. It was probably a Saxon royal hunting area and the manor is the first entry in the Hampshire folios of the Domesday Book - a great royal estate of 78½ hides, halfway between Winchester and Windsor or London. There are records of many visits by medieval kings. There was a palace in the town after the castle was built. Parliament met here in 1303 and Elizabeth I held Privy Council meetings in 1569 and 1591. *The George* was licensed in 1540 but has roof timbers dated to 1474 dendrochronologically. It was the posting house, Customs and Tax office and, until 1880, Petty Sessions were held in it. Odiham had a large Napoleonic Wars prisoner of war camp - near the chalk pit. *Odiham High Street* Barbara Wentworth Odiham Society 64pp

Odiham Airfield was opened in 1937 in response to the growing threat from Germany but the ceremony was performed by a Luftwaffe General, Erhard Milch. It is said the airfield was not bombed because the Luftwaffe earmarked it as their English HQ, but there is no evidence for this. Flying began here in1925 and the army subsequently held Air Cooperation camps each summer, the fields being used for grazing during the rest of the year. At present it is an RAF Chinook helicopter base for logistic support of the army.

Odiham Church, All Saints, is mainly of 13th century flint construction on the site of the Saxon Domesday Book church but it is much restored. Points of interest: the piscina which may be Saxon, 14th century pillars of the 3-arch north aisle contrasting with the 15th century pillars of the 4-arch south aisle, several brasses now on the walls (above the lectern, one of 1498 for William Goode, priest), the heavy-carved Jacobean pulpit, the RAF window in the tower arch. Two French gravestones near the north wall are for prisoners of the Napoleonic Wars. Outside the gate are the stocks. The pest house, at the SW corner, was built under a bequest of 1625 - an isolation hospital especially associated with plague. It was used as an almshouse 1780-1978.

Odiham Wharf opened in 1793 and grew to 3 acres with warehouses, offices and workshops near Colt Hill car park. The land owners met at *The George* in Odiham to finalise the sale of land for the canal in 1788 and John Pinkerton's sons lived in Odiham to supervise the building.

Pillboxes are World War II relics of the GHQ line which stretched from the Medway to near Gloucester to defend London and the Midlands. The line follows natural obstacles such as the Downs, canals and rivers.
Pillboxes - a study of UK defences 1940 Henry Wills 1985 Secker & Warburg 98pp

Pirbright is not in the Domesday Book but was probably cut from Woking Manor by Henry I for his son Robert, Duke of Gloucester. It was included in Katherine of Aragon's marriage portion. The Manor House is 16th century but there are records of a house in 1302; part of the moat is still visible. Some of the houses have Lord Pirbright's estate logo, P. The 17th century mill ground corn until the 1930s.   *The day before yesterday* Helen Yool 1973 56pp

Pirbright Church, St Michael and All the Angels, is Georgian but there was a church as early as 1200, deduced from a charter signed as witness by Jordan, parson of Pirefricth (facsimile in church). The grave of Stanley, the explorer, 1841-1904, is in the churchyard.

Pirbright Lodge was the home of Admiral John Byron (1723-1786) who explored the Pacific badly, fought a French fleet easily and became a grandfather poetically. As a midshipman he was stranded in Patagonia for six years and story has it that he set off to retire there but, coming to Pirbright, found it wild enough and stayed. The lane was the Chertsey to Farnham coach road.

Puttenham is not in the Domesday Book but the medieval church suggest is an ancient village; Wanborough is stated to have been two manors. The first mention of Puttenham is in 1199. The medieval village probably had three fields under strip cultivation and the south field would have given its name to Suffield Lane. The Pilgrims' Way went through the village and there was a pilgrims' fair in December. The oldest houses are the 15th century timber-framed Rosemary Cottage, Old Cottage and Winter's Farm. The brick houses, Hook Lane Farm, Street Farm and Farm Cottage, date from 1520-50. The oast houses below the church, now homes, ceased work in 1970, but there is still a hop field, the only one remaining in Surrey. The church, St John The Baptist, is Norman in origin, the south wall of the nave dating from about 1100 and the pillars from about 1160. The tower was added about 1400 but lost its spire to fire in 1735. The window between the porch and the tower is the re-used early 14th century east window. There is a brass of 1481, a memorial for Edward Cranford, Rector. *Puttenham under the Hog's Back* Ruth Dugmore 1972 Phillimore 155pp

Puttenham Common is worth exploring. It belongs to the Hampton Estate but is managed by Surrey County Council. An Iron Age hill fort, *Hillbury*, stands on the ridge. Roman bricks and tiles have been found nearby and Stone Age tools may still be found. General's Pond is said to have been made for General Oglethorpe (founder of the American colony of Georgia) who was Lord of the Manor in the 1740s. Lascombe, at the eastern edge, is a Lutyens house.

Puttenham Priory is a 17th century brick house with Palladian façade added by Thomas Park in the 18th century. It was never part of a monastery but the manor was willed to Newark Priory (near Woking) by Philippa de Melville in 1248. The priory would have drawn income from the profits of the land and an earlier house may have been occupied by its steward. In modern times the house has been a hospital and a business headquarters.

Rodsall Manor was probably the Domesday Book REDESSOLHAM, held in 1066 by the Saxon thegn, Tovi. The present house was built in 1680 and two rooms were added in 1724. The name probably derives from red soil.

The **Roman Pottery** mass-produced pots and tiles for 4 centuries from around AD 70. *Alice Holt ware* is found in excavations across southern England and occasionally in Northern France. The site came to light when the Portsmouth turnpike was built in the 1870s, cutting through spoil heaps of stratified broken pots over several acres. The underlying Gault clay, peat turf for kiln building and abundant fuel made the area suitable but it may have originated because of ancient skills for there was small scale production in the the Iron Age. 1st century kilns, about 1½m in diameter, were stacks of pots packed with wood and enclosed by a turf wall; only their bases are found in excavations; later kilns had stone walls. Experimental archæology suggests the best wood for fuel was straight lengths of 60cm, 5cm thick, and coppicing was probably used to produce them. Little charcoal has been found suggesting it was also traded.

Alice Holt/Farnham Roman Pottery Industry Lyne & Jeffries 1979 CBA Research 77pp

Rowledge parish straddles the county boundary. It was a Victorian creation to bring order to the rough inhabitants at the forest edge. Part was carved from the forest in Binsted Parish, Hants and part from Wrecclesham, Surrey. The malmstone church, St James', was consecrated in 1871. The *Cherry Tree* has Hampshire and Surrey bars. The name *Rowediche* appears in 1220, referring to the rough ditch dividing the counties.

Seale was *Bintungom*, an estate of 10 cassati, which Cædwal, King of Wessex, gave with Farnham to endow a minster or monastery as recorded in one of the earliest charters in 687. The name survives in Binton Farm and Wood. Seale is not in the Domesday Book as it was part of the great episcopal manor of Farnham. The malmstone and bargate church, St Laurence, started as a chapelry of the minster at Farnham. It was re-built in 1860 but the style of the re-used Norman door arch inside the porch is earlier than 1200. The Woodroffes memorialised were Lords of the Manor of Poyle (Tongham).

Seale Chalkpit is an SSSI both for its ecosystem and for its geology. The 50° dip can be seen on the underside of the plunging beds. Few chalk pits are still used. Farmers used to spread chalk to improve the acidic soils on the adjacent sands. It was roasted to make quick lime for mortar.

Street House in Thursley was the home of the London family that produced Sir Edwin Landseer Luytens, the architect 1869-1944. His first job at 19 was on the Thursley village shop and his early works were within bicycle range of Thursley. He completed 550 commissions: houses, memorials, cemeteries, palaces and bridges. His Surrey houses were succeeded by work all over the world: the British Embassy, Washington, the Viceroy's residence New Delhi, the British Pavilion at the 1900 Paris Exhibition, the Cenotaph.

Sir Henry Morton **Stanley** (1841-1904) of "Dr Livingstone, I presume" lived in retirement at *Furze Hill* nearby. He could be regarded as the greatest British overland explorer. BULA MATARI, *smasher of rocks*, was an epithet he acquired wielding a sledgehammer in the Congo. Illegitimate and brought up in a Welsh workhouse, he sailed to America, soldiered in the Civil War and joined the *New York Herald*. His great journalistic *coup* was finding Livingstone who had disappeared trying to prove Lake Tanganyika was the source of the Nile. They met at Ujiji in 1871. In a 2nd expedition he continued Livingstone's work, travelling down the Lualaba for 999 days to find it became the Congo, not the Nile. Employed by Leopold II of Belgium to build a chain of trading posts, Stanley became the creator of the Congo (now Zaire) and a catalyst for the carve up of Africa by the European powers. He might be considered the greatest British explorer but the savagery of his methods, the political turmoil he unleashed and his dishonesty denied him a place in Westminster Abbey.

Stanley: The Making of an African Explorer & *Sorcerer's Apprentice* F McLynn 1989 Constable

Swift's Cottage was the home of Stella who was tutored by Jonathan Swift and, as an adult, is suspected of being his secret lover. *Journal to Stella*, a compilation, is in effect, Swift's diary.   Edited by Harold William OUP 1948 1169pp

The **Tarn** is the lowest of a ladder of ponds stretching a mile up the valley which were Repton's work of the 1800s when he landscaped Hampton Park. The millpond, next down the valley, is probably medieval.

Thursley was not a Domesday Book manor, probably being part of Witley Manor then, but the Saxon walls of the church indicate there was already a settlement. The village lies on the old London to Portsmouth road. Several old and picturesque cottages surround the church. See Street House.

Thursley Church, St Michael & All Angels, has a massive oak frame inserted around 1500 to support the bell turret. Points of interest: Saxon windows and wafer oven in the north wall of the chancel, a Saxon window in the nave; Saxon font; sundial on the tower; several 18th century table tombs; the graves of the murdered sailor (facing the war memorial) and John Freeman the poet.

Thursley Common is a National Nature Reserve of English Nature. It has the richest dragonfly fauna in Britain and all the British reptiles. Uncommon birds nest here: Dartford warbler, hobby, nightjar, stonechat, snipe, curlew and reed bunting. As well as dry heath there is raised bog with the irregular holes of old peat diggings. The Cricklestone and Thor's Stone are ancient boundary marks; Thor's probably acquired its romantic name from *The Broom-squire*. The long mound with the board walks is on the Saxon boundary of AD 688, when the Wessex king, Cædwalla, gave the Farnham lands to the Bishop of Winchester.

Tileries is a house on the site of a tilery and brickworks that exploited the London Clay. The works opened in 1885 and closed a hundred years later.

Tilford has a few picturesque or ancient houses on the Farnham road but is a largely modern ribbon development on the Elstead Road. The triangular green is particularly splendid when cricket is in progress on its undulating turf. The church at the south end is mid-Victorian. The timber framed Tilford Institute is the Lutyens village hall built in 1893. The oak at the north corner is ancient but not the Kingeoak documented in 1147 as a boundary mark for a virgate of land given by Henry de Blois, Bishop of Winchester, to Waverley Abbey.

The two **Tilford bridges** across the South Wey and the main Wey are 13th century ironstone structures, similar to the Waverley Mill, Elstead, Eashing & Unsted bridges - assumed to be innovations of the Waverley monks. When the one by the car park was restored in 1998, extra arches were found in the bank.

Tilford Mill gave its name to the bridge but its exact position is unknown. It was demolished in the 1850s but there are documentary records of a flour mill here in 1679 and a fulling mill in 1307.

The **Tongham Railway** was the original route for London trains to Farnham. It opened from Guildford in 1849 and was extended to Alton in 1852. There were stations at Tongham and Ash Green and a spur to the Aldershot gasworks for coal. Ash Green was the only station near Aldershot when the army arrived. Traffic declined after the Pirbright-Aldershot LSWR branch opened in 1870 but the line did not close until 1961.   The Tongham Railway P A Harding 1994 32pp

Waggoners Wells was earlier known as Wakeners Wells. The streams are headwaters of the River Wey (S). Tradition has it the ponds were for a hammer mill. Henry Hooke, Lord of the Manor of Bramshott, was in dispute with the commoners of Ludshott and Bramshott in the middle of the 17th century for damming the valley, which took away common land. Around 1670, he was supplying shot (cannon balls) from his works, Bramshott Hammer, 3 miles downstream at Passfield and it seems likely the ponds were his reserve of power, hence the belief they were hammer ponds. Water mills drove hammers, bellows and turning machinery. Sussex was the main iron smelting area of Britain in the Roman and medieval times having the ore, charcoal and water power. The adjacent forested areas of Surrey and Hampshire had forges and foundries which bought in and re-worked blooms and pig-iron from Sussex.
The Iron Industry of the Weald H Cleere & D Crossley 1995 Merton Priory Press 425pp

Wanborough village is on a spring where the water emerges from the chalk at the top edge of the London Clay. It was the Saxon manor WENEBERGE in the Domesday Book. Its Lord, Leofwin, according to tradition, was killed at the battle of Hastings. A few days later it was laid waste by a Norman army skirting London prior to the English capitulation. It was bought for £100 in 1130 as a grange for the new Waverley Abbey whose lay-brothers would have worked it, hence local place names with *monk* or *greyfriars*. Wanborough Illinois got its name when Morris Birkbeck, tenant farmer, emigrated to America in 1817 with workers from Wanborough and Puttenham. A church was recorded in the Domesday Book. The present church, St Bartholomew's, was built in the 12th century with defensive strength. Wanborough Manor house was the farm house of the one-farm manor. It bears the date 1527 when it still belonged to Waverley Abbey but architectural detail suggests it was built 1650-70. During World War II it was the SOE (Special Operations Executive) training centre for French Resistance agents and it flits through the espionage novels of Ted Allbeury. Trainees were not allowed to speak English so local people called them "foreigners". *Wanborough from White Barrow to World War* Gillian Drew 1993 28pp

Wanborough Great Barn is Surrey's most important medieval aisled barn. Guildford Museum arranges open days and group visits. 1388 is the building date suggested by tree ring data but the octagonal pillars were cut early in that century, presumably for an earlier building. The barn was in agricultural use until about 1988 and was fully restored in 1997. It was not a tithe barn.

Wanborough Roman Temple at Christmaspie came to light through the activities of metal detectorists which depressed the price of Roman coins. Thousands were lost to site robbers and a rescue excavation was mounted in the 1980. It was a square timber building of 2nd century age. An adjacent Celtic temple with pre-Roman coins was excavated in 1999. This was of 1st century construction and built of flint.

Watts Chapel in the cemetery is extraordinary. It was financed by Watts and designed by his wife Mary (d 1938) in Italian Romanesque style. The bricks and decorative gesso panels were made at the terracotta works by 74 villagers.

Watts Gallery is free and open most afternoons. It displays 500 works of the painter and sculptor George Watts. The adjacent buildings were a studio and factory for terracotta ware until 1956 using the underlying Gault clay. The 1950's TV potter's wheel interlude was filmed here. A Roman house excavated 1914 in the Watts' garden at *Limnerlease* yielded three coins dated 313-378.

Watts, George Frederick, 1817-1904, sold 5 shilling portraits at the age of 16 and served as the House Artist to the British Ambassador in Florence. His best known work is *Physical Energy* in Kensington Gardens. He was a friend of Dickens, Thackeray and Tennyson. His first wife was Ellen Terry.

Waverley Abbey was the first Cistercian house in England, founded in 1128 by William Giffard, the 2nd Norman Bishop of Winchester, with monks from Normandy. Greyfriars worked as farmers and avoided wealth and towns. The monastery church, started in 1203, was one of the most splendid, like the extant Fountains. After the dissolution of 1536, the abbey was acquired by Sir William FitzWilliam who sold the timber and lead. Much of the stone went to build Loseley House. The *Annals of Waverley*, now in the British Museum, end in mid-sentence in 1291 and are an important source for historians.

Waverley Abbey H Brakespear Surrey Archæological Society 101pp

Waverley Abbey House was built in the mid 18th century for Thomas Orby Hunter. William Cobbett writes of working in the garden as a child. In World War I it was an annex of Cambridge Military Hospital, Aldershot. Since 1987 it has been the headquarters of the CWR which organises courses and publications in Christian education.

Well is a hamlet surrounded by arable country. It was an estate cut out of Long Sutton Manor in the 12th century. The road is the Harow Way.

Willey Mill first appears in the Bishop of Winchester's pipe roll of 1207 when the bailiff had to account for 10 shillings rent and it is probably one of the six Domesday Book mills of Farnham. The name *weo léage* appears in the charter of 909 probably deriving from *weoh* a temple or idol and *leah* clearing.

Wimble Hill is both the eminence and the hamlet. The ridge is the chalk outcrop continued from the Hog's Back across the Blackwater Valley. The hamlet was the site of a late 18th century orphanage. The succeeding hospital functioned until 1976. The lane is the Harow Way and is deep sunk in places. It forms the parish boundary of Crondall and Bentley, a clue that it was in being when King Cædwalla granted Bentley to the church of Farnham in 688.

Yagden Hill, 83m/272 feet, is on the end of the great spur from Kettlebury Hill capped by gravel which is a terrace of the proto-Blackwater River.